real life ENTERTAINING

real life ENTERTAINING

EASY RECIPES AND UNCONVENTIONAL WISDOM

JENNIFER RUBELL

PHOTOGRAPHS BY CHRIS TERRY

WILLIAM MORROW
An Imprint of HarperCollinsPublishers

HarperCollins books may be purchased for educational, business, or sales promotional use. For information please write: Special Markets Department, HarperCollins Publishers, 10 East 53rd Street, New York, NY 10022.

FIRST EDITION

Designed by Vertigo Design, NYC

Printed on acid-free paper

LIBRARY OF CONGRESS CATALOGING-IN-PUBLICATION DATA
Rubell, Jennifer.
    Real life entertaining : easy recipes and unconventional wisdom / Jennifer Rubell.—1st ed.
        p. cm.
    ISBN-13: 978-0-06-077847-7
    ISBN-10: 0-06-077847-4
1. Quick and easy cookery. 2. Entertaining. I. Title.
    TX833.5.R676 2006
    641.5'55—dc22
                                                    2005044381

06 07 08 09 10 ❖ / TP 10 9 8 7 6 5 4 3 2 1

TO MY PARENTS, DON AND MERA

You have always been my model for real life

CONTENTS

ACKNOWLEDGMENTS

HARRIET BELL, it has meant so much to me that you fell in love with this book and supported me every step of the way through its creation. You are courageous and incredible.

Carrie Bachman, David Sweeney, Leah Carlson-Stanisic, Alison Lew, Will Staehle, Roberto de Vicq de Cumptich, Michele Corallo, Kelly Jones, Jenny Leff, Roscel Garcia, Lucy Baker, and everyone at HarperCollins, thank you for your hard work, support, and belief in this project. Alan Nevins, thank you for taking on *Real Life* and putting it into such capable hands. Mindy, you're a star.

My thanks to all the people who made the *Real Life* photo shoot so magical: above all Chris Terry—whose heart is as sweet as his eye—Danny, Liza, Cari, Elodie, the Rubell Hotels staff, Liliana Zarif, Mark Coetzee, Juan Valadez, and everyone at the Rubell Family Collection. Jung Kim, you were a goddess in a pinch, and I'm deeply grateful.

Jason, thank you for helping me get here, in every way. I know that without you this project, and so many of the things that are meaningful to me, would never exist. Thank you Michelle, Samuel, Ella, and Olivia for making Jason so happy, and for being constant inspirations to me.

Mitchell Kaplan, I was deeply moved by your early support of this book, and continue to be awed by your generosity. Brian Antoni, you are the root of my success in all things. Sarah Harrelson, thank you for giving me the opportunity that set all this in motion, and for being a great friend in the process. Deborah Needleman, Zoe Wolff, Dana Cowin, Kim Upton, Ingrid Abramovich, and Silvana Nardone, thank you all for your encouragement, enthusiasm, and belief along the way. Eve and Peter, thank you for rooting for me so sincerely and substantially over the years. Larry Schwarz, thank you for having me throw every one of your birthday parties since sixth grade, and for loving everything I've ever cooked. And Jean-François, *merci d'avoir toujours cru*. Mario Batali, Peter Elliot, and Jonathan Morr, you are all gods.

Daniel, it's hard to imagine that I ever had a real life without you. Thank you for transforming a fantasy into our reality.

To the [Signet] Society, where my entertaining flame was kept alive and nourished during my years at Harvard, I raise a very loving cup to you.

And to Steve, the ultimate host, I miss you.

INTRODUCTION

WHEN I WAS NINE YEARS OLD, my parents invited their diamond-dealer friend Buzzy Baumgold over for dinner one summer night. I insisted on playing hostess, preparing, cooking, and serving a full three-course meal. I ironed the napkins and set the table with the prettiest plates my parents owned. The dinner started with tall wineglasses filled with tomato juice, a slice of lemon perched on each rim, which I thought was very fancy at the time. I made some kind of lasagna (in the middle of the summer!) that took me all afternoon to assemble and cook. I don't remember the exact dessert, but I know there was one, and I know I baked it from scratch. The adults played along with my efforts, ironed napkins in laps, exhibiting their finest table manners while I did my best to approximate a fancy restaurant dinner. I thought the evening was a major success, and the next day, my smug assessment was reinforced: A package arrived from Buzzy's office, and inside was a heart-shaped diamond ring.

I don't remember anything else about being nine years old.

From those early tomato-juice-as-appetizer days until now, entertaining has always been a significant part of my life. After college, I moved to Miami, to open a group of boutique hotels with my family. At one hotel, the Albion, I wrote a continuous bedtime story that was placed on every guest's pillow at night. At another, the Beach House, I created an employee fund so the staff could buy little gifts for guests they particularly liked.

I was always looking for that human connection, that place where a hotel stops being a business and starts feeling like a home. I knew our guests by name. I remembered their children's names, what clothes they wore, and what kind of music they listened to. The menus I created for our hotel restaurants featured food our guests liked to eat—modern, bright, honest home cooking.

I lived in each of the hotels for a year when they first opened, and in between I created homes of my own. After spending my days overseeing staff and taking care of guests, what I craved was simplicity and intimacy: unpretentious, easy, comfortable evenings at home with friends. Cooking was a major part of these evenings, though never a major undertaking. The food I made was rustic and simple, ridiculously easy to prepare but still gorgeous and delicious when it arrived at the table. Everything was always served family style, and everyone participated: Someone brought wine, another person brought dessert, a few friends helped with the dishes at the end of the night.

I developed a particular way of entertaining for insanely busy lives that's long on style and short on fuss. Everything I cook is from scratch, but nothing is complicated. Excitement comes less from exotic, hard-to-make dishes than from interesting combinations of familiar ingredients, simply prepared.

A FEW YEARS AGO, Sarah Harrelson, an editor at the *Miami Herald,* came to my house for a party, and the next day she asked me to write a story about my entertaining style for the newspaper's new magazine, *Home & Design*. That first story was called "5 Friends, $100 to Spend, 1 Hour to Cook and 1 Pan to Clean," and it received such positive reader response that Sarah asked me to turn it into a column. I've been writing that column—and articles for newspapers and magazines around the country—ever since, with readers constantly asking me for more recipes, more ideas, more ways to entertain that fit in with their hectic lifestyles. I realized that the solutions I had developed for my own fast-paced whirlwind life—how I integrated home, family, food, and friends—addressed some of the common anxieties of people across the country.

The old rules of entertaining just don't apply anymore. We simply don't have the time, staff, or inclination to follow them, yet so many of us are not entertaining at all because we're still afraid to break those rules. We need a new model. We need to make our homes—and the way we entertain in them—an extension of our modern, casual, informal lifestyles. Yes, you're allowed to use paper napkins (or even paper towels) instead of ironed linen napkins. Yes, you can serve everything all at once instead of shuffling back and forth to the kitchen for a formal three-course meal. Yes, it's okay to invite people just a couple of days before.

Real Life Entertaining is the exact opposite of picture-perfect, made-for-TV, high-anxiety entertaining. It's creative, rule-free, and low-stress. No social pressure. No holy-grail quest for The Perfect Meal. It's personal and flawed, idiosyncratic and improvisational. It's time for you to be you, surrounded by people you like, not worried about who's going to pay the check or order the wine. It's private time, at home, in a judgment-free bubble where your guests bring drinks or dessert or music, and the party unfolds as it will.

Next time you think about throwing some elaborate, high-stress party, give real life entertaining a try instead. Pick up the phone, invite over some friends, and whip up some of the easy recipes in this book. I can't guarantee any diamond rings, but I promise you'll feel like a star.

real life ENTERTAINING

drop-in DINNERS

THE essentials

THE BASIC CONCEPT

You know those nights when you head out to a local restaurant with a few friends on the spur of the moment? It's not about getting all dressed up or going to the swankiest spot in town. You don't care about all that. You just want to catch up with people you feel connected to over a bowl of pasta or a quick casual meal.

Well, that's what these dinners are all about, only instead of going out to some mediocre local joint, you get together at your place, where you can sit for as long as you like, eat good food you prepare yourself, and relax in your own private world. I call these drop-in dinners because whether your friends live right next door or all the way across town, these nights have an impromptu quality. Everyone's in jeans or sweatpants. It's just a regular weeknight, and you're taking the time to be with friends and enjoy each other. The house can be a mess, the kids can be playing under the table, and everyone can roll up his or her sleeves and clear the table together. Some people might not even call dinners like this "entertaining," but for me they're the essence of real life entertaining: sharing your day-to-day life with people you care enough about to invite into your home.

IDEAL NUMBER OF GUESTS

4

WHO TO INVITE

Neighbors, friends; parents, siblings, and children; anyone on your personal speed dial.

MINIMUM ACCEPTABLE ADVANCE NOTICE

20 minutes

WHAT TO TELL YOUR FRIENDS TO BRING

Anything you forgot! Charcoal for the barbecue. A six-pack. That box of penne you could've sworn was in the cabinet. You shouldn't be shy about asking close friends to pick up whatever you need.

SETTING THE MOOD

Give someone a stack of dishes to put out on the table. Hand someone else the silverware. Open a bottle of wine and let your friends pour for themselves. The key to making drop-in dinners feel right is not overdoing anything—the less it feels like a "company" dinner, the better.

DRINK OF CHOICE

Inexpensive wine, beer, iced tea, or just plain water.

ULTIMATE SIGN OF SUCCESS

Everyone does the dishes together.

WHY I COOK THE MEALS IN THIS CHAPTER

They're quick and inventive without being fussy, and they use ingredients that I always have on hand. I use techniques that cut down on cooking time, from not peeling the garlic cloves for Rustic Chicken Night to recycling a quick garlic marinade for two different dishes in the Miami Shrimp Grill. Also, the recipes use as few pots and pans as possible, so I'm not left with an hour's worth of dirty dishes to wash after preparing an easy meal in 20 minutes.

RUSTIC CHICKEN *night*

CHICKEN WITH GARLIC CLOVES AND ROSEMARY

WARM MUSTARDY POTATOES

WATERCRESS AND GOAT CHEESE SALAD WITH DIJON VINAIGRETTE

CHICKEN WITH GARLIC CLOVES
AND ROSEMARY

SERVES 4

2 pounds (9 or 10) skinless, bone-less chicken breast cutlets

1 teaspoon kosher salt

1 teaspoon freshly ground black pepper

½ cup extra virgin olive oil

4 rosemary sprigs

4 heads garlic, broken into cloves but not peeled

½ teaspoon red pepper flakes, optional

Leaving garlic cloves un-peeled is a great trick for imparting maximum flavor with minimum effort. Keep chicken cutlets in the freezer for a ready-to-go meal when you don't have time to shop.

PLACE A WIDE, heavy-bottomed pan over high heat. Season the chicken breasts on both sides with the salt and pepper. When the pan is hot, add the olive oil, rosemary, and garlic cloves. Cook, stirring occasionally, until some of the garlic looks like it's just about to burn, about 10 minutes. With a slotted spoon, transfer the garlic and rosemary to a large plate (don't worry about the stray leaves left in the pan). Keeping the pan over high heat, place 3 or 4 of the chicken cutlets in the pan, being careful not to overcrowd them. Cook for 2 minutes, then flip and cook for 1 to 2 minutes more, depending on the thick-ness of the cutlets. Remove from the pan, and place the chicken on top of the garlic on the plate. Repeat with the remaining chicken cutlets. Remove the pan from the heat. Press down the pile of chicken cutlets with the back of a spoon to release the garlic juices, then return everything to the pan, garlic on top. Sprinkle with red pepper flakes, if desired, and serve in the pan.

PARTY TRICK
Cut down on the number of dirty dishes in the sink by serving food right out of the pan it was cooked in. Added bonus: a rustic look on the table.

WATERCRESS AND GOAT CHEESE SALAD WITH DIJON VINAIGRETTE

SERVES 4

1½ teaspoons Dijon mustard

1½ teaspoons red wine vinegar

3 tablespoons extra virgin olive oil

2 bunches watercress (about 4 large handfuls), stems removed, torn into bite-sized pieces

4 ounces goat cheese, crumbled

A pinch of freshly ground black pepper

IN A SALAD BOWL, combine the mustard and vinegar and stir with a spoon. Slowly drizzle in the olive oil a little at a time, stirring vigorously and adding more only after the previously added oil has been completely incorporated. The mixture should maintain a thick consistency. Add the watercress and toss well. Sprinkle the goat cheese on top and add the pepper.

Tossed with one of my all-time favorite kitchen staples, classic Dijon vinaigrette, this salad takes only a couple of minutes to make. The vinaigrette uses ingredients that should be in your pantry, and tastes infinitely better than any store-bought dressing.

PARTY TRICK

To make mismatched dishes feel more pulled together, collect them in just one or two colors. Buy odd dishes wherever you find them—thrift stores, yard sales, and Internet auctions—commit to one color palette, and when you set the table everything will work well together.

WARM MUSTARDY POTATOES

SERVES 4

2 pounds (10 to 15) small red-skinned potatoes

1 tablespoon Dijon mustard

1 tablespoon white wine vinegar

½ cup extra virgin olive oil

¼ teaspoon freshly ground black pepper

1 tablespoon drained capers

PLACE THE POTATOES in a pot of salted water and bring to a boil. Boil until the potatoes are tender when pierced with a fork, 15 to 20 minutes. In a serving bowl, combine the mustard and vinegar and stir with a spoon. Slowly drizzle in the olive oil a little at a time, stirring vigorously and adding more only after the previously added oil has been completely incorporated. The mixture should maintain a thick consistency throughout. Add the capers. Drain the potatoes and toss in the bowl with the dressing, breaking them roughly into thirds with a spoon while mixing them thoroughly with the dressing.

These potatoes are tossed with a vinaigrette similar to the one on the watercress salad, but with more mustard and some capers thrown in. Prepare the dressing in the serving bowl to avoid using extra dishes.

WEEKDAY pasta and salad

With pasta, especially one as rich as this, you don't need anything more than a simple salad alongside.

PENNE GORGONZOLA

ARUGULA SALAD WITH BALSAMIC PRUNE VINAIGRETTE

PENNE GORGONZOLA

SERVES 4

One 1-pound box penne

¼ cup extra virgin olive oil

2 tablespoons butter

2 teaspoons honey

1 ½ teaspoons lemon juice

2 cups crumbled Gorgonzola

1 teaspoon freshly ground black pepper

BRING A LARGE POT of salted water to a boil. Add the penne and cook for one minute less than the package's lowest estimate, or until the penne is a little firmer than al dente. Drain the pasta and return it to the pot, over low heat. Immediately add all of the remaining ingredients and stir well until the cheese is melted. Serve immediately.

Could it be any easier? This recipe is almost as quick as re-heating a jar of store-bought sauce, but the results are creamy, tangy, and downright elegant. Add Gorgonzola to your weekly grocery list and you'll always have what you need on hand.

ARUGULA SALAD WITH BALSAMIC PRUNE VINAIGRETTE

SERVES 4

1 teaspoon Dijon mustard

1 teaspoon balsamic vinegar

3 tablespoons extra virgin olive oil

1 tablespoon prune juice

2 bunches arugula, washed well

IN A SALAD BOWL, combine the mustard and vinegar and stir with a spoon. Slowly drizzle in the olive oil a little at a time, stirring vigorously and adding more only after the previously added oil has been completely incorporated. The mixture should maintain a thick consistency. Add the prune juice and stir to combine. Add the arugula to the bowl and toss well.

Oh, poor prune juice! Everyone makes fun of it, yet it's such a useful thing (in so many ways). I've added a bit to this vinaigrette to cut the balsamic vinegar's acidity—you barely notice it's there, but it imparts a subtly tangy note that's perfect for peppery arugula.

PARTY TRICK

If you have a salad spinner and don't have time to go shopping right before a party, here's a great way to make sure your arugula will be ready when you are. When you get home from the store, wash the arugula, spin it dry, then put the whole spinner in the fridge. Being dry in a humid environment is any salad green's idea of nirvana—it'll be perfectly crisp and ready to go for days.

SALMON STEAKS
and potatoes

CUCUMBER RELISH WITH MINT AND BASIL

ROASTED SALMON STEAKS WITH MUSTARD SEEDS AND FRESH DILL

GOLDEN YUKON GOLDS

ROASTED SALMON STEAKS WITH MUSTARD SEEDS AND FRESH DILL

SERVES 4

Four 8-ounce salmon steaks, about
1 ¼ inch thick

1 tablespoon honey

1 tablespoon extra virgin olive oil

¼ teaspoon kosher salt

2 teaspoons mustard seeds

1 tablespoon chopped fresh dill

1 lemon, cut into wedges

Mustard seeds give the salmon a kick of flavor without that typical prepared mustard taste. Think of them as adult Pop Rocks: little bursts of wasabi-like flavor that come with every bite.

PREHEAT THE OVEN to 375°F.

PLACE THE SALMON STEAKS in a single layer on a sheet pan. Drizzle the honey and olive oil on both sides of the salmon and, with your hands, rub the mixture into the fish. Sprinkle with the salt, mustard seeds, and dill. Place in the oven and cook for 20 minutes without turning. Serve with lemon wedges.

CUCUMBER RELISH WITH MINT AND BASIL

SERVES 4

1½ cups yogurt

2 cucumbers, cut in half length-wise, seeded, and sliced ⅛ inch thick

1½ tablespoons chopped mint

1½ tablespoons chopped basil

1 tablespoon lemon juice

½ teaspoon red pepper flakes

1 teaspoon minced garlic

½ teaspoon kosher salt

½ teaspoon freshly ground black pepper

Inspired by the cooling raitas of Indian cuisine, this relish has a bright, herbal flavor to go with the salmon. It also goes nicely with lamb, or serve it as a dip for Sesame-Mint Pita Chips (page 107).

COMBINE ALL THE INGREDIENTS in a serving bowl and mix well. If there's time, let the relish sit for an hour.

Conventional WISDOM

Cloth napkins are a must at any kind of dinner party.

real life WISDOM

If you're too much of a perfectionist about entertaining, you're never going to do it. Paper napkins—or even paper towels—are fine for a drop-in dinner. I also like to use freshly laundered dishcloths.

GOLDEN YUKON GOLDS

SERVES 4

5 Yukon gold potatoes, cut into
¾-inch cubes

½ cup extra virgin olive oil

2 teaspoons kosher salt

1 teaspoon freshly ground black
pepper

6 rosemary sprigs

I make these little golden babies almost every week. They're fabulous with steak, too.

PREHEAT THE OVEN to 375°F.

PLACE THE POTATOES on a sheet pan. Sprinkle with the olive oil, salt, and pepper, adding the rosemary sprigs on top. Toss well with your hands, then spread out into a single layer. Place the potatoes in the oven and cook for 10 minutes. Remove the pan and flip the potatoes with a spatula. Return the pan to the oven and cook for another 10 minutes, or until the potatoes are a deep golden brown.

PARTY TRICK

If you're making two things in the oven at the same time and they're cooking at the same temperature (like the salmon and potatoes in this meal), use the biggest pan you can find, start the longer-cooking item first, then add the shorter-cooking item at the appropriate time. You'll cut down on dirty dishes, and the pan will look gorgeous enough to bring right to the table.

MIAMI shrimp grill

GRILLED SHRIMP WITH GARLIC AND CITRUS

SERVES 4

1½ pounds medium-large shrimp

2 garlic cloves

4 tablespoons extra virgin olive oil

1 teaspoon kosher salt

½ teaspoon freshly ground black pepper

1 orange, sliced into wedges

1 lemon, sliced into wedges

1 lime, sliced into wedges

PREPARE A MEDIUM-HOT GRILL or place a grill pan over high heat. Peel the shrimp, leaving on the tail and the section right before the tail. Make a shallow cut all the way down the back and pull out the vein. Wash and dry the shrimp. In a bowl, combine the garlic, olive oil, salt, and pepper. Add the shrimp and toss to coat. Place the shrimp in a single layer on the grill and cook until the bottom starts to turn pink, about 2 minutes. Using tongs, flip the shrimp, being careful not to let them fall through the grill (though frankly, a few will probably get away). Cook until the other side turns pink, about 2 more minutes. Serve immediately, with the sliced citrus alongside, and encourage everyone to squeeze a little of each fruit on top.

I often serve food that requires my guests to participate in the preparation, and this dish is the perfect example. A good part of its flavor comes from squeezing three kinds of citrus fruit on top of the shrimp once it comes to the table, a job that even my most kitchen-phobic friends are happy to do.

Conventional WISDOM

Pans are for cooking, platters are for serving.

real life WISDOM

Some vessels intended for cooking make the prettiest serving pieces. After grilling the shrimp, I transfer them to a beautiful earthenware baking sheet for serving.

BUTTERED CORN WHEELS

SERVES 4

6 ears corn, shucked

4 tablespoons extra virgin olive oil

1½ tablespoons butter

½ teaspoon sea salt

PREPARE A HOT GRILL or place a grill pan over medium-high heat.

CUT OFF THE ENDS OF THE CORN with a sharp, heavy knife. Cut the remaining ears crosswise into 1-inch rounds by pressing hard and straight down. Toss the corn and olive oil in a bowl, then place the corn on the grill, cut side down. Cook for 8 minutes, then turn and cook for another 8 minutes. Remove from the grill, then toss in a serving bowl with the butter and salt.

Slicing ears of corn into rounds makes them a little more elegant and a lot easier to eat.

PARTY TRICK

No one ever wants to be the first to eat with his or her hands. When you're serving something, like the shrimp and corn here, which would be great as finger food, set the example yourself. Pick up that first shrimp, and your guests are guaranteed to follow.

PAPAYA AND CILANTRO SALAD

SERVES 4

2 papayas, peeled, seeded, and cut into ¾-inch cubes

Juice of 1 lime (about 2 tablespoons)

¼ cup chopped cilantro

1½ teaspoons freshly ground black pepper

½ teaspoon kosher salt

A pinch of cayenne pepper, optional

PLACE ALL THE INGREDIENTS in a serving bowl and toss well.

Cooling papayas make a unique salad, and their tropical sweetness matches shrimp perfectly. It's essential to use ripe papayas, and the best way to pick them out is by feel—they should be firm, but with just a little give, like a tomato.

sit-down DINNERS

THE essentials

THE BASIC CONCEPT

Forget all the associations you have with the phrase "sit-down dinner." These aren't stuffy, formal, boring dinners with frou-frou food and more stress than should ever be allowed inside a private home. They're the exact opposite of all that. Everything is served family style around a big table, so there's no running back and forth to the kitchen. You can actually enjoy yourself rather than worrying about burning the next course or whether your seating arrangement is successful. You become a full participant at the table.

At my house, these dinners go on for hours, ending up with a collection of empty wine bottles on the table and the kind of animated conversation that makes new friends out of total strangers. See what happens at yours.

IDEAL NUMBER OF GUESTS
8

WHO TO INVITE
A good mix: some work friends; a few people you've known since childhood; a couple you recently met and want to know better. Sit-down dinners are great for cementing a new friendship or fitting an old friend into a busy schedule.

MINIMUM ACCEPTABLE ADVANCE NOTICE
5 days

WHAT TO TELL YOUR FRIENDS TO BRING
Have everyone bring a bottle of wine; ask close friends to bring dessert.

SETTING THE MOOD
Don't fuss about having just the right china, glasses, and silverware—mixing and matching tableware is fine. For instant atmosphere arrange a bunch of different candles on the table—that glow makes everything (including you) look divine.

DRINK OF CHOICE
The wine your friends brought; water with some lemon or cucumber floating in it; a little grappa or dessert wine if you're in the mood.

ULTIMATE SIGN OF SUCCESS
People exchanging phone numbers before they walk out the door.

WHY I COOK THE MEALS IN THIS CHAPTER
Every single one of them allows me to sit at the table the entire time. All of the food is prepared before anyone sits down, and in many cases, before any guests arrive. Instead of dressing up food with time-consuming techniques and hard-to-find ingredients, I add a little something unexpected that makes a major difference: fennel seeds tossed into sautéed peppers, tangy pickles in an orzo salad, dried figs for a sweet note to mashed potatoes.

To save time, I often make the main dish and a side in the same pan, and then separate them just before serving. The Garlic-Roasted Chicken with Carrots and Parsnips and Roast Leg of Lamb with Chickpeas and Burnt Onions are two examples. In both cases, the juices from the meats give the vegetables a deep, flavorful richness.

SIMPLE, ELEGANT,
so south of france

The carrots and parsnips cook in the same pan as the chicken, creating an extra side dish with no extra effort.

ENDIVE WITH BLUE CHEESE AND WALNUTS

GARLIC-ROASTED CHICKEN WITH CARROTS AND PARSNIPS

GARLIC-ROASTED CHICKEN WITH CARROTS AND PARSNIPS

SERVES 8

4 bone-in chicken breasts with wings attached, washed and patted dry with paper towels

7 large carrots, cut into 2-inch sticks

7 parsnips, cut into 2-inch sticks

2 whole heads garlic, broken into cloves but not peeled, plus 3 garlic cloves, minced

⅔ cup extra virgin olive oil

2 teaspoons kosher salt

1 teaspoon freshly ground black pepper

Leaves from 5 thyme sprigs

This dish has all the hominess of a roasted whole chicken, but without the fuss and mess of carving.

PREHEAT THE OVEN to 400°F.

LINE A SHEET PAN with aluminum foil. Place the chicken, carrots, parsnips, and whole garlic cloves on top and drizzle with the olive oil. Sprinkle with the salt, pepper, and thyme. Toss until the chicken and vegetables are well coated. Arrange so that the vegetables are in a single layer on the bottom, then rub the chicken with the minced garlic and place it, skin side up, on the pan.

PLACE THE PAN in the oven and cook for 45 minutes. Baste the chicken with the pan juices (tilt the pan and spoon the juices over the chicken with a serving spoon) and cook for another 15 minutes. To test for doneness, cut into the thickest breast to make sure it is cooked through. Serve.

Conventional WISDOM
For company, prepare an impressive dish that you wouldn't serve to your family.

real life WISDOM
No matter how sophisticated someone is, everyone craves honest home cooking. If your best dish is a perfect roast chicken, then serve it to your guests.

ENDIVE WITH BLUE CHEESE AND WALNUTS

SERVES 8

2 teaspoons Dijon mustard

2 teaspoons white wine vinegar

¼ cup extra virgin olive oil

6 heads endive, quartered length-wise

1 cup (about 5 ounces) crumbled blue cheese

1 cup (about 4 ounces) walnut pieces

Whole heads of endive are cut lengthwise into quarters, remaining attached at the base, an easy technique for a fresh, modern look. If you're not a blue cheese fan, replace it with goat cheese, feta, or shaved Parmesan.

PLACE the mustard and vinegar in a serving bowl and stir well to combine. Slowly drizzle in the olive oil, stirring until all the oil has been incorporated before adding more. Add the endive to the bowl and toss with the dressing. Sprinkle the blue cheese and walnuts on top.

PARTY TRICK

When you mix something directly in its serving bowl, give the inner edge a swipe with a moistened paper towel just before bringing the bowl to the table for a more finished look.

SUMMER tuna spectacular

SEARED TUNA WITH OLIVES AND TOMATOES

SERVES 8

¼ cup plus 2 tablespoons extra virgin olive oil

¾ cup (about 4 ounces) pitted Kalamata olives, roughly chopped

2 tablespoons capers, chopped if large

8 plum tomatoes, chopped into ½-inch dice (4 cups total)

5 thyme sprigs

Four 12- to 14-ounce tuna steaks, 1 inch thick

2 teaspoons freshly ground black pepper

Seared tuna is one of the easiest dishes to prepare at the last minute. The key is to place the tuna steaks in a really hot pan; turn the steaks when a bottom crust has formed.

PLACE A WIDE, heavy-bottomed pan over high heat. Add ¼ cup of the olive oil, the olives, capers, tomatoes, and thyme. Cook, stirring occasionally, until a thickish sauce is formed but the tomatoes still retain their shape, about 5 minutes. Transfer the sauce to the edges of your serving platter, and wipe the pan clean with a paper towel. Place the pan back over high heat. While it's heating, rub the tuna steaks with the remaining olive oil and the pepper. When the pan is smoking hot, place the tuna steaks in it in a single layer (do this in two batches if necessary). Cook the tuna **without touching it** for about 3 minutes, until the fish has changed to a white color halfway up the sides. Flip and cook until just a tiny bit of pink remains on all sides, another 2 minutes (for medium rare). Remove the tuna to a cutting board and cut it into ¼-inch slices. Arrange them in the center of the serving platter.

THREE-PEPPER STIR-FRY

SERVES 8

¼ cup extra virgin olive oil

4 garlic cloves, peeled and cut in half

2 red bell peppers, sliced into ½-inch strips

2 yellow bell peppers, sliced into ½-inch strips

2 orange bell peppers, sliced into ½-inch strips

1½ teaspoons fennel seeds

1 teaspoon kosher salt

½ teaspoon freshly ground black pepper

¼ teaspoon red pepper flakes, optional

PLACE A WIDE, heavy-bottomed pan over high heat. When the pan is hot, add the olive oil and garlic. Cook, stirring occasionally, until the garlic just starts to turn golden, about 2 minutes. Add the peppers and cook, stirring occasionally, for 7 minutes. Add the fennel seeds, salt, and pepper, and cook, stirring often and scraping up seeds from the bottom, until the peppers are softened but not mushy, about 7 more minutes. Sprinkle with red pepper flakes, if desired, and serve, warning your guests to pick out the garlic cloves.

The inspiration for this dish came from the sausage and pepper heroes I used to eat as a kid at the San Gennaro festival in New York's Little Italy. The sausage always had garlic and fennel in it, which gave the peppers a bright, Mediterranean taste. Here, I've taken out the sausage, but left that garlic-fennel-pepper combination for a perfect summer side.

Conventional WISDOM

You should keep track of what you serve guests at each dinner party so you won't replicate the meal in the future.

real life WISDOM

If you serve something and it's a success, make it your signature dish. You'll find that your friends start talking about "Zoe's great orzo" or "those fabulous roasted potatoes Ethan makes." Some of the world's greatest hosts are known for one great dish.

ORZO WITH LEMON, FETA, CURRANTS, AND . . . PICKLES

SERVES 8

1 pound orzo

⅓ cup extra virgin olive oil

Juice of 1 lemon

1 cup (about 4 ounces) crumbled feta

¼ cup chopped parsley

10 cornichons, chopped

½ cup (about 2 ounces) dried currants

1 teaspoon freshly ground black pepper

BRING A POT OF SALTED WATER to a boil. Add the orzo and cook it until it's al dente, about 6 minutes. Drain and rinse with cold water for 30 seconds, until the orzo has come to room temperature. Place in a serving bowl and add the remaining ingredients. Stir well to combine.

PARTY TRICK

One of the hardest things to get right when entertaining is timing: How do you make sure everything's ready at the same time? One solution is to serve most of the food at room temperature, and then bring out your one main dish piping hot. When that dish is ready, everyone sits down.

This room-temperature salad is a happy accident that has become one of my signature dishes. One day, I was having a few people over for dinner and at the last minute, some out-of-town friends called to say they were in Miami for one night only. To stretch the meal, I put together a quick pasta salad, using some left-over ingredients in the fridge, and this orzo was the result. It's sweet, sour, and tangy, all at the same time, with the pickles adding just the right crunch.

A REAL roast

Roasting chickpeas directly in the pan with the lamb creates a wonderfully rich same-pan side

ROAST LEG OF LAMB

SHREDDED CARROT SALAD WITH CURRANTS AND CUMIN

CHICKPEAS AND BURNT ONIONS

ROAST LEG OF LAMB WITH CHICKPEAS AND BURNT ONIONS

SERVES 8

4 yellow onions, thinly sliced

Four 15.5-ounce cans chickpeas, drained and rinsed (see Note)

½ cup extra virgin olive oil

One 6- to 7-pound bone-in leg of lamb

1 tablespoon kosher salt

1 tablespoon freshly ground black pepper

There's something about bringing a big chunk of meat still on the bone to the table that feels feastlike, even if it's one of the easiest things to make in the world. Roast some canned chickpeas and sliced onions along with the meat; they will caramelize in the rich lamb juices.

PREHEAT THE OVEN to 350°F.

PLACE THE ONIONS, chickpeas, and ¼ cup of the olive oil on a sheet pan. Toss well to coat with the olive oil. Move the vegetables to the sides of the pan, leaving room for the lamb in the center. Rub the lamb with the remaining olive oil, then sprinkle it on all sides with the salt and pepper. Place in the center of the pan and roast for 20 minutes *per pound* for medium-rare. Let the lamb sit for 10 minutes before carving. Serve, with the chickpea-onion mixture on the side.

NOTE: If the chickpeas you find are in different-sized cans, don't worry. A little bigger or smaller won't make any difference at all.

Conventional WISDOM

The busier someone is, the more notice he or she needs before being invited to a party.

real life WISDOM

Busy people are often much easier to pin down at the last minute than months in advance. Don't be shy to call someone even hours before a party to see if they're free. If they are, they'll really appreciate it.

SHREDDED CARROT SALAD WITH CURRANTS AND CUMIN

SERVES 8

6 cups (about 8) shredded carrots

Juice of ½ lemon

½ cup extra virgin olive oil

1 teaspoon ground cumin

¼ teaspoon sugar

½ cup (about 2 ounces) currants

1 teaspoon kosher salt

PLACE ALL THE INGREDIENTS in a serving bowl and stir to combine. If you have time, let the salad sit for an hour or so. Otherwise, it's great as is.

While the Middle Eastern flavors here go nicely with the lamb, I frequently serve this easy carrot salad at picnics, brunches, and barbecues, and even keep some in the fridge as a healthy snack.

PARTY TRICK

You don't need place cards, but seating a table well can make the difference between a really fun evening and one that falls a little flat. If you're busy finishing something in the kitchen, recruit your significant other or best friend to do the job. Some good general guidelines (of course, there are no absolute rules): couples across from each other, potential love connections side by side, and the host right in the middle.

STEAK, surprising spuds, and heavenly sprouts

MASHED POTATOES WITH FIGS AND PARMESAN

GRILLED SKIRT STEAK WITH ORANGE-MINT CHIMICHURRI

THYME-ROASTED BRUSSELS SPROUTS

GRILLED SKIRT STEAK WITH ORANGE-MINT CHIMICHURRI

SERVES 8

2 cups chopped parsley

¼ cup chopped mint

½ cup extra virgin olive oil

Juice of 1 lemon

Zest of 1 orange

Juice of 1 orange

3 skirt steaks (3 to 3¾ pounds)

1 tablespoon kosher salt

1 tablespoon coarsely ground black pepper

PREPARE A MEDIUM-HOT GRILL. Make the chimichurri: Combine the parsley, mint, olive oil, lemon juice, orange zest, and orange juice in a bowl and stir well. Set aside. Sprinkle the steaks with the salt and pepper and place on the grill. Cook for 3 minutes, then flip and cook for another 3 minutes for medium-rare. Slice thinly across the grain and serve, with the chimichurri on the side.

I discovered chimichurri at Argentinian steak houses in Miami, where the uncooked parsley-based green sauce is usually packed with garlic and served with Flintstone-sized steaks. My version is a little milder, with the intensity of garlic replaced by the wonderfully bright flavor of both orange juice and orange zest.

Conventional WISDOM

Have a full bar, so that guests will have their preferred drink available to them.

real life WISDOM

Full bars cost a lot of money to maintain and can be a mess without a bartender, and most guests are happy to drink whatever you serve them anyway. Offer your guests wine and water or, if you're really ambitious, one specialty cocktail made for the occasion.

MASHED POTATOES WITH FIGS AND PARMESAN

SERVES 8

7 dried figs

10 medium Yukon gold potatoes, cut into 1-inch cubes

4 tablespoons butter

½ cup extra virgin olive oil

1¼ cups grated Parmesan

½ teaspoon kosher salt

½ teaspoon freshly ground black pepper

While the combination here may sound contemporary, this dish is inspired by a classic Venetian ravioli stuffed with—you guessed it—figs and potatoes.

BRING A POT OF WATER TO A BOIL. Place the figs in a bowl and cover with boiling water ladled from the pot. Soak for about 10 minutes. Place the potatoes in the pot. Boil them until they're fall-apart tender, 10 to 12 minutes, then drain and place in a serving bowl. Remove the figs from the soaking water **but don't throw the soaking water away**. Chop the figs and add them to the potatoes with ¼ cup of the soaking liquid, the butter, olive oil, Parmesan, salt, and pepper. Mash everything with a fork until it's well combined but still a little lumpy (home style).

Conventional WISDOM

Always serve only easily likable foods at dinner parties. Don't take any risks with foods that might turn people off.

real life WISDOM

Trust your taste. If you like something unusual, take a chance and serve it to your friends, too. People are often more open than you think, and you might just introduce them to a new favorite.

THYME-ROASTED BRUSSELS SPROUTS

SERVES 8

Three pints Brussels sprouts

½ cup extra virgin olive oil

15 thyme sprigs

½ teaspoon kosher salt

½ teaspoon freshly ground black pepper

PREHEAT THE OVEN to 375°F.

CUT A THIN SLICE off the bottom root end of the Brussels sprouts and discard. Halve the Brussels sprouts lengthwise by cutting through the flat end, and wash them. Dry the sprouts well and place them on a sheet pan with the olive oil and thyme. Sprinkle with the salt and pepper, then toss until coated. Spread the Brussels sprouts out in a single layer, pick out and discard any loose leaves, and place the pan in the oven. Cook for 30 to 35 minutes without turning, until they are a deep golden brown in places (even if certain parts look a little burnt, that tastes great).

Everyone thinks they hate Brussels sprouts until they try these, and then they can't stop eating them. Cutting each sprout in half is more work than I'm usually inclined to do, but the payoff is massive: Once roasted, the outside leaves become crispy while the insides are tender, with a sweet flavor.

41

get-TOGETHERS

THE essentials

THE BASIC CONCEPT

When I hear the phrase "cocktail party," I picture an elegant affair with tuxedoed waiters carrying around silver platters of hors d'oeuvres and bartenders serving well-dressed guests any mixed drink they request. Guests are physically uncomfortable, standing on sore feet while trying to balance an hors d'oeuvre in one hand and a colorful cocktail in the other. And cocktail parties aren't just total nightmares for guests, they are also time-consuming and needlessly expensive for the host.

I prefer to host what I call get-togethers, parties featuring a single well-chosen drink and food that's a focal point but not a full-on meal. With everyone drinking exactly the same thing, there's a wonderful feeling of conviviality, reinforced by food that's visually arresting enough to get people to cluster around it. The food begins conversations and creates energy. There's a sense of shared experience, of discovery, of excitement, and most important, much less anxiety for the host.

IDEAL NUMBER OF GUESTS
12

WHO TO INVITE
These are the most dressed-up parties in this book (while being pretty low-stress for you), so if you have some friends you really want to impress, now's the time to invite them: Bosses, clients, in-laws, fussy friends, and potential significant others are all good bets (though maybe not at the same time).

MINIMUM ACCEPTABLE ADVANCE NOTICE
2 days

WHAT TO TELL YOUR FRIENDS TO BRING
If your music collection is spotty, have someone bring a few jazz tracks.

SETTING THE MOOD
There's something about plastic glasses that takes the fun out of a get-together, not to mention how bad they are for the environment. Buy one or two dozen inexpensive all-purpose wine-glasses at a restaurant supply store. If you don't want to spend the money, try rummaging through your cupboards: I've served wine in everything from jelly jars to hand-me-down champagne flutes.

DRINK OF CHOICE
One of my favorite things about these parties is that you don't have to stock a full bar. Each one of these parties suggests a spe-cific drink: red wine with Bruschetta; Spiced Pear Bellinis with open-faced sandwiches; Beer Cocktails with wings, and champagne with tasting spoons.

ULTIMATE SIGN OF SUCCESS
The shyest person in the room makes a new friend.

WHY I MAKE THE GET-TOGETHERS IN THIS CHAPTER
I make each one for a different reason. The bruschetta is basically do-it-yourself, which is lots of fun and a great way to bring people together. The open-faced sand-wiches look amazingly beautiful for something so simple to pre-pare. The wings are healthier, more contemporary versions of an American classic—and nothing goes better with football. And the tasting spoons are pure elegance, without the fuss of passed hors d'oeuvres.

RED WINE and bruschetta

Some easy-to-drink wines I love with bruschetta: Chianti, Côtes du Rhône, Shiraz, or Chilean Merlot.

BASIC BRUSCHETTA

SERVES 12

One 8-inch-round loaf rustic
Italian bread, cut into twelve
½-inch-thick slices

½ cup extra virgin olive oil

1 to 2 garlic cloves, halved (leave
the skin on)

PREHEAT THE OVEN to 375°F.

PLACE THE BREAD in a single layer on a sheet pan. Drizzle the bread with the olive oil, then flip and drizzle the other side. Bake until the bread starts to turn golden on the bottom, about 10 minutes. Turn and cook for another 5 minutes until golden brown. Remove from the oven. Rub the top of each slice a few times with a halved garlic clove. Serve with one or several of the following toppings.

It's amazing what a little garlic and olive oil can do to a piece of toast. Buy the best rustic bread you can find, and resist piling on too much topping. (And if you don't have time to make your own, store-bought pesto or tapenade is great in a pinch.) Rather than assembling the bruschetta myself, I put out a big bowl of toasts with the toppings alongside and let my guests do it, which makes much less work for me, and includes everyone in the fun of participating.

CLASSIC TOMATO, BASIL, AND GARLIC
TOPPING

MAKES ABOUT 3 CUPS

7 to 8 plum or heirloom tomatoes, roughly chopped

10 basil leaves, finely chopped

1 garlic clove, minced

¼ cup extra virgin olive oil

1 teaspoon kosher salt

½ teaspoon freshly ground black pepper

This topping is best when made with lush, ripe tomatoes at the height of summer. And if you can find colorful heirloom tomatoes, all the better.

COMBINE ALL THE INGREDIENTS in a serving bowl and stir well. Let the topping sit at room temperature for 30 minutes to allow the flavors to develop.

PARTY TRICK

Stack a few plain white paper towels on top of one another and cut them into four squares for easy modern cocktail napkins.

CANNELLINI AND ROSEMARY TOPPING

MAKES ABOUT 3 CUPS

½ cup extra virgin olive oil

4 garlic cloves, minced

Two 19-ounce cans cannellini beans, drained and rinsed

Juice of ½ lemon

1 tablespoon chopped rosemary

½ teaspoon kosher salt

1 teaspoon freshly ground black pepper

PLACE A LARGE PAN over medium-low heat. When the pan is hot, add the olive oil and garlic. Cook, stirring occasionally, until the garlic just begins to turn golden, about 2 minutes. Add the beans and ¾ cup water. Turn the heat to high until the liquid comes to a boil, then lower to a simmer and cook, mashing slightly with the back of a spoon every once in a while, until the mixture resembles a chunky thick paste, about 20 minutes. Add the lemon juice, rosemary, salt, and pepper. Serve either warm or at room temperature.

This classic Tuscan combination has the ideal bruschetta-topping texture: smooth enough to spread on bread, but chunky enough so you can really get the flavor of the beans. It's also great to serve as a dip with carrot sticks, celery, or sliced fennel.

ZUCCHINI AND MINT TOPPING

MAKES ABOUT 3 CUPS

¾ cup extra virgin olive oil

2 garlic cloves, chopped

6 zucchini, cut into ¼-inch dice

1 tablespoon chopped mint

1 teaspoon red pepper flakes

1 teaspoon kosher salt

1 teaspoon freshly ground black pepper

Serve this topping hot right out of the pan or from a bowl at room temperature.

PLACE A LARGE PAN over medium-high heat. When the pan is hot, add the olive oil and garlic. Cook, stirring occasionally, until the garlic just begins to turn golden, about 2 minutes. Add the zucchini and cook, stirring occasionally, until the zucchini has softened but maintains its shape, about 10 minutes. Remove from the heat, add the remaining ingredients, and stir well to combine.

Conventional WISDOM

A good host offers ready-to-eat appetizers for arriving guests.

real life WISDOM

Letting people participate in the process makes them feel included, and is a great conversation starter. Arrange the toppings in bowls and have people assemble their own bruschetta.

BELLINIS AND open-faced sandwiches

SPICED PEAR BELLINIS

HONEYED PEAR, BLUE CHEESE, AND WALNUT SANDWICHES

CUCUMBER SANDWICHES

TRUFFLED EGG SALAD SANDWICHES

SPICED PEAR BELLINIS

MAKES 30

5 cinnamon sticks

Two 33.8-ounce bottles of pear nectar (about 9½ cups)

2 teaspoons ground cardamom

⅓ cup sugar

6 bottles Prosecco or other sparkling wine, chilled

PLACE THE CINNAMON on a cutting board, and with the flat side of a large knife, press down to break the sticks. Put the broken sticks in a pot and add the pear nectar, cardamom, and sugar. Place over high heat and cook, stirring occasionally, until the mixture comes to a boil. Turn off the heat and cover. Let it sit for at least an hour, then pour it into a pitcher and refrigerate for at least 3 hours. For each serving, pour the spiced nectar into a champagne flute about two fingers high and fill with Prosecco.

I created these for my childhood friend Larry's thirty-fifth birthday party, and everyone adored them. Make the pear mixture a few hours before the party to give it time to chill.

PARTY TRICK

To figure out how many cocktails to make, use common sense: Think about the people who will be at your party, and how much they typically drink. One cocktail a night? Two? Five? Whatever the average number is, multiply it by the number of guests coming and throw in a few extra drinks just in case. This works better than any general guidelines—you know your friends (and their drinking habits) better than anyone else.

TRUFFLED EGG SALAD SANDWICHES

MAKES 12

6 eggs

¼ cup mayonnaise

2 teaspoons truffle oil

¼ teaspoon kosher salt

6 tablespoons butter, at room temperature

6 sourdough rolls, sliced in half

12 small leaves (from about 2 heads) butter lettuce

2 tablespoons thinly sliced chives

The lettuce cups give these sandwiches a fresh look, and the truffle oil adds an earthy flavor. Take the butter out of the fridge before you start anything else.

PLACE THE EGGS IN A POT and cover with cold water. Place over high heat and bring to a boil. Remove from the heat, cover, and let sit for 6 minutes. Run the cooked eggs under cold water, then peel. Cut the eggs into ¼-inch chunks and place in a bowl. Add the mayonnaise, truffle oil, and salt, and stir well to combine. Butter each half-roll and place a lettuce leaf on top to form a cup (the butter will keep it in place). Divide the egg salad evenly among the lettuce cups (about 2 tablespoons each) and sprinkle each with some chives.

PARTY TRICK

Give your table a good cleaning and arrange your hors d'oeuvres geometrically right on the tabletop for one of my favorite modern presentations.

CUCUMBER SANDWICHES

MAKES 12

1 cucumber, sliced in half length-wise, seeds removed, and cut into ¼-inch cubes

1 teaspoon kosher salt

6 tablespoons butter, at room temperature

6 white rolls, sliced in half

1 tablespoon chopped fresh dill

IN A BOWL, combine the cucumber and salt. Generously butter each half-roll and sprinkle with a pinch of salt. Divide the cucumber mixture evenly among the roll halves and sprinkle the dill on top.

I love the flavor of those crustless little cucumber sandwiches fancy hotels serve at afternoon tea, but they're way too labor-intensive to make at home. Try this easy-to-assemble version instead.

HONEYED PEAR, BLUE CHEESE, AND WALNUT SANDWICHES

MAKES 12

2 tablespoons cold butter, plus 6 tablespoons butter, at room temperature

2 pears (do not peel), cut into ⅛-inch slices

2 tablespoons honey

A pinch of kosher salt

6 French rolls, cut in half

1½ cups (about 9 ounces) crumbled blue cheese

1 cup (about 4 ounces) walnut halves

This sandwich is a riff on a classic French salad, but of course bread makes everything better.

PLACE A HEAVY-BOTTOMED PAN over high heat. Add the cold butter. After it has melted and the foam subsides, add the pears and stir to coat. Spread them out as much as possible and cook for 3 minutes, without moving them, until the pears have softened but not lost their shape. Add the honey and salt and cook, without moving them, for 4 more minutes. Turn off the heat and let the pears cool. Divide the softened butter evenly among the roll halves and spread thinly. Place 4 to 5 slices of cooked pear on each half-roll, then sprinkle with the blue cheese. Top with the walnut halves.

BEER COCKTAILS and wings

BEER COCKTAILS

Beer (any kind of lager is fine)

Lemonade

Grenadine, optional

A RECIPE DOESN'T GET ANY EASIER THAN THIS: Fill a glass halfway with lemonade, and the rest of the way with beer. For a pink drink, add a splash of sweet grenadine.

PARTY TRICK

Thrift stores are great sources for vintage glassware (that's where I got the glasses you see in the photo). Don't worry about finding matching sets—different beer steins, for example, look great together and help guests keep track of whose is whose.

Known as shandies in England and *pressions* in France, beer cocktails are rarely found in the beer-loving United States, yet they're the perfect accompaniment to chicken wings. They're light, low in alcohol, refreshing, and a whole lot prettier than a stand-alone brew.

Sure, you can make lemonade from scratch, but I'm perfectly happy to use the premade variety, setting it out with a six-pack of beer and a bottle of grenadine so guests can assemble these beer cocktails to their liking.

MASTER ROASTED CHICKEN WING RECIPE

SERVES 12

30 chicken wings (about 4 pounds)

¼ cup extra virgin olive oil

1½ teaspoons kosher salt

1 teaspoon freshly ground black pepper

PREHEAT THE OVEN to 400°F.

LINE A SHEET PAN with aluminum foil (nonstick aluminum foil is great if you can find it). Place the wings on the pan in a single layer. Drizzle with the olive oil and toss to coat. Sprinkle with the salt and pepper on both sides. Place in the oven for 50 minutes without turning. Remove from the oven and carefully peel the wings off the aluminum foil with tongs.

There's nothing easier to make than these chicken wings. Don't turn them, don't look at them, just put them in the oven and get on with the rest of your day. And then toss them with one of the following. So simple.

PARTY TRICK

At get-togethers, try not to serve anything that requires a plate (they're so hard to juggle with a glass in hand, and such a pain to wash afterward). For chicken wings, I put a big roll of paper towels on the table.

CILANTRO PESTO WINGS

SERVES 12

1 bunch cilantro, stems removed

½ bunch parsley, stems removed

½ cup extra virgin olive oil

4 garlic cloves

½ cup (about 2 ounces) walnut pieces

1 tablespoon lime juice

½ teaspoon freshly ground black pepper

½ teaspoon kosher salt

Master Roasted Chicken Wing Recipe (page 64)

Great on wings, this pesto is also delicious on everything from sandwiches to salads to roasted meats.

PLACE THE CILANTRO, parsley, and olive oil in a blender. Pulse on high until the herbs are well puréed, about 30 seconds. Add the remaining ingredients and pulse again until fully incorporated, about 30 seconds. Pour in a bowl, add the wings, and toss to coat.

SUPER-SPICY CHICKEN WINGS WITH BLUE CHEESE DRESSING

SERVES 12

1 stick butter (¼ pound), cut into pieces

½ cup Tabasco

Master Roasted Chicken Wing Recipe (page 64)

Blue Cheese Dressing (recipe follows)

Celery sticks

PLACE THE BUTTER AND TABASCO IN A BOWL. Add the wings while still hot from the oven. Toss well to coat and serve with blue cheese dressing and celery sticks.

Coated with equal parts butter and Tabasco, these wings aren't going to win any anticholesterol awards—and they just might set your mouth on fire for the next couple of hours—but nothing goes better with football.

BLUE CHEESE DRESSING

MAKES ABOUT 2 CUPS

1½ cups (about 9 ounces) crumbled blue cheese

½ cup sour cream

½ cup mayonnaise

2 teaspoons Worcestershire sauce

½ teaspoon freshly ground black pepper

PLACE ALL THE INGREDIENTS in a bowl and stir well, mashing the blue cheese until combined.

Make a double batch and keep some in the fridge. It's great drizzled on a wedge of iceberg.

THAI CHICKEN WINGS

SERVES 12

½ cup honey

1 teaspoon Worcestershire sauce

Zest of 2 limes

Juice of 1 lime (about 2 table-spoons)

2 tablespoons soy sauce

2 garlic cloves, finely minced

1 tablespoon chopped cilantro

2 teaspoons red pepper flakes

1 teaspoon freshly ground black pepper

1 teaspoon kosher salt

Master Roasted Chicken Wing Recipe (page 64)

This sauce is also great on a batch of cooled pasta for a quick Asian noodle salad.

PLACE ALL THE INGREDIENTS except the wings in a bowl and stir well. Pour ⅓ cup of the mixture over the wings while still hot and toss to coat. Serve the rest on the side as a dipping sauce.

CHAMPAGNE AND tasting spoons

POACHED SALMON WITH CUCUMBER RELISH SPOONS

SEARED FLANK STEAK WITH BLACK BEAN SALSA SPOONS

TOMATO-OREGANO SALAD WITH FRESH FETA SPOONS

POACHED SALMON WITH CUCUMBER RELISH SPOONS

MAKES 12

1 tablespoon kosher salt

One 5-ounce salmon fillet (as thin as possible), skin removed

½ cucumber, cut into ⅛-inch dice

2 tablespoons white vinegar

1 teaspoon sugar

1 tablespoon chopped fresh dill

½ teaspoon freshly ground black pepper

Poached salmon is so easy to make, and you can keep it chilled in the fridge for lunch salads, summertime dinners, or a quick hors d'oeuvre like this one.

PLACE 2 INCHES OF WATER and the salt in a wide pan over high heat. When the water comes to a boil, add the salmon, turn off the heat, and cover tightly with aluminum foil. Let sit for 8 to 11 minutes (the thicker the piece of salmon, the longer it needs to sit), then remove from the water and, with a spoon, break it apart into 12 bite-sized pieces. Meanwhile, combine the cucumber, vinegar, sugar, dill, and pepper in a bowl and toss well to combine. Divide the cucumber mixture among 12 Chinese soup spoons and place a piece of salmon on top of each one.

Conventional WISDOM

Cocktail parties are the time to pull out all the stops and serve really luxurious foods.

real life WISDOM

At large get-togethers the numbers can quickly add up. Save the lobster, caviar, foie gras, and smoked salmon for intimate dinners with someone you love (or skip them altogether and buy some new shoes)!

SEARED FLANK STEAK WITH BLACK BEAN SALSA SPOONS

MAKES 12

¾ teaspoon kosher salt

1 teaspoon freshly ground black pepper

¼ pound flank steak

¾ cup canned black beans, drained and rinsed

1 plum tomato, seeded and chopped

2 tablespoons roughly chopped cilantro

Juice of ½ lime

1 jalapeño, finely chopped, optional

PLACE A HEAVY-BOTTOMED PAN over high heat. Sprinkle ½ teaspoon of the salt and ½ teaspoon of the pepper evenly on both sides of the meat. When the pan begins to smoke, place the steak directly in the dry pan and cook, without touching, until you see the edge start to brown, about 2 minutes. Turn and cook for another 2 minutes. Transfer to a cutting board and let the meat rest for at least 5 minutes. Meanwhile, combine the beans, tomato, cilantro, lime juice, jalapeño, if desired, and remaining salt and pepper. Divide this mixture evenly among 12 Chinese soup spoons. Slice the steak into 12 bite-sized pieces and top each spoon with a slice.

This Tex-Mex combo makes a great dinner for one if you skip the spoon-assembly part.

PARTY TRICK

My favorite tasting spoons are the inexpensive porcelain or plastic ones used in Chinese restaurants. They're available at houseware stores.

Conventional WISDOM

A good host is constantly preparing and serving.

real life WISDOM

Finish cooking and setting up everything for a get-together before the first guest walks through the door. That way, you can enjoy the party—and all the cocktails you want—without worrying that you'll forget something in the kitchen.

TOMATO-OREGANO SALAD WITH FRESH FETA SPOONS

MAKES 12

3 plum tomatoes, seeded and chopped

8 Kalamata olives, finely chopped (about 2 tablespoons)

2 teaspoons finely chopped oregano

Juice of ½ lemon

1 teaspoon extra virgin olive oil

¼ teaspoon freshly ground black pepper

3 ounces feta, cut or crumbled into 12 bite-sized pieces

If you're not serving this Greek-inspired vegetarian option immediately, add the olives at the last minute to avoid discoloring the tomatoes.

COMBINE THE TOMATOES, olives, oregano, lemon juice, olive oil, and pepper in a bowl. Toss well, then divide among 12 Chinese soup spoons. Top each with a piece of feta and serve.

CREATING YOUR OWN SPOON COMBINATIONS

The great thing about the tasting spoon concept is that you can literally put anything inside. When I don't feel like cooking at all, I love throwing together these store-bought combinations: coleslaw and pulled barbecued chicken, salsa and precooked shrimp, cranberry sauce and smoked turkey, vichyssoise and snipped chives, and gazpacho and croutons.

Whether you go the store-bought route or try some homemade ideas, here are some tips. Spoon combinations have two layers. The first one is a bit of soup, relish, or other condiment that slides easily out of the spoon when eaten. The top layer should be the opposite of the bottom—a bite of chicken or shrimp, or some crunchy croutons—something that contrasts in color, texture, shape, and taste to what's underneath.

Foods that work at room temperature are best, since the spoons will sit out for a while.

brunch

THE essentials

THE BASIC CONCEPT

I never used to invite people over for brunch. Recently, however, my friends started having babies, and in those first few weeks when they were homebound with their newborns, I found myself going over to their houses and cooking brunch on weekends. I'd invite a couple of our close friends, go shopping for the ingredients, arrive at their doorsteps with my bags of groceries, and whip up something quick and delicious for everyone. The baby would be asleep, or in someone's lap, and we'd all sit around the table eating our eggs and toast feeling like some kind of wonderful extended family.

Through these brunches, I discovered something that's true at any stage—or nonstage—of family life. The late morning is the exact opposite of what I feared: It is, in fact, one of the most intimate times of the day, especially if it's a Sunday (plus, if there are any small children in your social set, you've probably discovered how much easier it is to integrate them with adults during the day). Brunchtime is warm, cozy, and a great time to feel connected to people who really mean something to you.

IDEAL NUMBER OF GUESTS
8 to 12

WHO TO INVITE
Anyone you consider family

MINIMUM ACCEPTABLE ADVANCE NOTICE
At least a week, since Sundays tend to get booked up

WHAT TO TELL YOUR FRIENDS TO BRING
Orange juice, pastries, babies

SETTING THE MOOD
Set everything up as a buffet in the kitchen. Let your friends serve themselves right from the pan.

DRINK OF CHOICE
There's only one drink that's absolutely mandatory at brunch, and that's coffee. Even if you don't drink it, keep in mind that we live in a nation of major caffeine addicts, and you might see a side of your friends you never wanted to see if you don't give them their fix.

ULTIMATE SIGN OF SUCCESS
No one wants to leave.

WHY I COOK THE MEALS IN THIS CHAPTER
They take no time and very little effort, and all the ingredients can be purchased in advance. The Eggs and Onions in the New York Brunch are made with two staple ingredients found in any kitchen. The quiche in the Simple Chic Brunch is shockingly simple to assemble. The baked Baguette French Toast lets you serve this brunch classic all at once. And the Tex-Mex Breakfast Mess is downright addictive (not to mention a great use for stale tortilla chips).

NEW YORK brunch

COFFEE

ORANGE JUICE

TOASTED BAGELS WITH CREAM CHEESE AND CAPERS

EGGS AND ONIONS

EGGS AND ONIONS

SERVES 8

¼ cup extra virgin olive oil

2 onions, sliced ¼-inch thick

16 large eggs, beaten

¼ teaspoon kosher salt

¼ teaspoon freshly ground black pepper

HEAT A WIDE, heavy-bottomed pan over medium-high heat. Add the olive oil and onions. Cook, stirring occasionally, for 20 minutes until most of them are dark brown (it's okay if you start to see a few little ones turning almost black before then. Just keep going). Add the eggs, salt, and pepper and cook, stirring every minute or so, for about 5 minutes. Remove from the heat when the eggs are very loosely set (they'll continue to cook). Bring the pan straight to the table and serve.

My grandfather Phil used to make this dish for my brother and me every Saturday morning. The key is getting the onions really sweet by caramelizing them until they are deep brown; only then are the eggs added. Bring the pan straight to the table to keep the eggs warm while everyone digs in.

PARTY TRICK

Bring the toaster into the dining room, or wherever you are serving, with a big platter of sliced bagels, so everyone can toast his or her own without disrupting the conversation.

SIMPLE CHIC brunch

CRUSTLESS HAM AND CHEESE QUICHE

SERVES 8

1 teaspoon butter

1 tablespoon flour, plus more for flouring the pie plate

2 cups heavy cream

3 large eggs

½ teaspoon kosher salt

¼ teaspoon freshly ground black pepper

¼ teaspoon ground nutmeg

8 ounces ham, cut into ¼-inch dice

6 ounces thick-sliced Gruyère, cut into ¼-inch strips

Since this quiche is crustless, it eliminates just about all the carbs of a traditional quiche, as well as the bother of making a crust. Whip it up a day or two in advance; it reheats perfectly.

PREHEAT THE OVEN to 375°F. Butter and flour a 9-inch pie plate. In a bowl, beat together with a fork the cream, eggs, salt, pepper, and nutmeg until they are just combined, then pour the mixture into the pie plate. In a separate bowl, toss the ham and Gruyère with the 1 tablespoon flour. Sprinkle this mixture onto the cream mixture in the pie plate and pat it down with your hands until everything is at least partially submerged. Place the pie plate in the oven and bake for 30 minutes until it is golden on top. Let it cool to room temperature (about ½ hour) and serve. Or make it ahead of time and reheat it in a 325°F oven for about 20 minutes.

PARTY TRICK

One way to make people feel comfortable is to let them help you. Have a friend serve the quiche. Ask someone else to pour the orange juice. You're not imposing on them; you're including them in your world.

APPLE AND FENNEL SALAD

SERVES 8

6 tablespoons mayonnaise

3 tablespoons buttermilk

1 teaspoon white vinegar

Zest of 1 lemon

Juice of ½ lemon

1 tablespoon chopped fresh dill

¼ teaspoon kosher salt

½ teaspoon freshly ground black pepper

2 red Delicious apples, *not* peeled, thinly sliced into sticks

2 large fennel bulls, fronds removed, thinly sliced into sticks

COMBINE THE MAYONNAISE, buttermilk, vinegar, lemon zest, lemon juice, dill, salt, and pepper in a serving bowl and stir well to combine. Add the apples and fennel as you slice them (to prevent browning), then toss everything well to coat before serving.

This salad got its start on a Sunday morning when I had invited a bunch of friends over and had been, um, let's say, a bit neglectful about shopping. I found the apples and fennel in the bottom drawer of my fridge, and after fiddling around with them a bit came up with this combination. I'm not much of a mayo fan, but here it serves as the base for a tangy, light dressing that really ties everything together.

PARTY TRICK

Not enough water pitchers around? Use clean, empty wine or juice bottles instead. Run the bottles under hot water to loosen the labels, rub them off, and fill 'em up.

MINTY SUGAR SNAP PEAS

SERVES 8

¼ cup extra virgin olive oil

2 pounds sugar snap peas, strings removed

3 tablespoons finely chopped mint

1 tablespoon lemon juice

1 teaspoon kosher salt

½ teaspoon freshly ground black pepper

PLACE A WIDE, heavy-bottomed pan over medium-high heat. When the pan is hot, add the olive oil and sugar snap peas. Cook, stirring occasionally, until the peas are crisp-tender, 10 to 12 minutes. Turn off the heat and add the remaining ingredients. Toss well to combine before serving.

Peas and mint are a classic combination, especially in the spring. The key to this quick stir-fry is to add the mint at the very end so it retains its brightness and fresh herbal flavor.

FANCY french toast brunch

BAGUETTE FRENCH TOAST

SERVES 12

1 teaspoon butter

4 large eggs

¼ cup milk

½ teaspoon ground cinnamon

¼ teaspoon salt

1 baguette, cut on the bias into 1-inch slices

Maple syrup

PREHEAT THE OVEN to 375°F. Butter a nonstick sheet pan.

IN A BOWL, beat the eggs, milk, cinnamon, and salt. Place the bread slices in the egg mixture, turn to coat well on both sides, and place on the sheet pan in a single layer. Place in the oven and bake for 5 minutes, then turn and cook for another 4 minutes until golden brown. Serve with maple syrup.

Preparing French toast for a crowd can be a problem. Unless you have three skillets going simultaneously, the first batch is inevitably cooked and cold before you get the next egg-soaked bread slices into the pan. By using the oven instead, you can prepare this favorite in ten minutes from start to finish.

PARTY TRICK

If you don't have a coffeemaker, or if yours isn't large enough for a crowd, mix some instant espresso powder with milk and ice instead for on-the-spot iced café con leche. Start with a tablespoon per glass, then add more if you want it stronger.

BABY SPINACH AND ALMOND SALAD

SERVES 12

2 tablespoons Dijon mustard

2 tablespoons balsamic vinegar

1 cup extra virgin olive oil

1 teaspoon freshly ground black pepper

1 pound baby spinach

¾ cup sliced almonds

The almonds in this recipe give the dressing an almost grainy quality, which makes a great contrast to the silkiness of the spinach leaves.

IN A LARGE SALAD BOWL, combine the mustard and vinegar and stir with a spoon. Slowly drizzle in the olive oil a little at a time, stirring vigorously and adding more only after the previously added oil has been completely incorporated. The mixture should maintain a thick consistency throughout. Add the pepper and stir once more. Add the spinach to the bowl and toss with the dressing. Top with almonds and serve.

FAMILY brunch

TEX-MEX
BREAKFAST
MESS

SALSA

PEANUT
BUTTER AND
JELLY YOGURT

PINEAPPLE,
STRAWBERRY,
AND BANANA
SALAD

TEX-MEX BREAKFAST MESS

SERVES 12

2 tablespoons butter

18 large eggs, lightly beaten

½ teaspoon kosher salt

1 teaspoon freshly ground black pepper

5 tomatoes, cut into ½-inch chunks

Two 15-ounce cans black beans, drained and rinsed

1 cup (about 4 ounces) shredded Cheddar

1 large handful tortilla chips, the staler the better

¼ cup sour cream

Salsa (page 90)

A breakfast mess is basically scrambled eggs with the kitchen sink thrown in. In this version, broken tortilla chips give the eggs a big lift in body and texture. There's no hang-over in the world this dish can't fix.

IN A WIDE, heavy-bottomed pan, melt the butter over medium-high heat. Pour in the eggs and sprinkle with the salt and pepper. Cook, stirring occasionally, until it seems like about three-quarters of the eggs are set, 3 to 5 minutes. Add the tomatoes, black beans, and Cheddar. Crumble the tortilla chips into the pan. Cook for about 10 minutes, until the eggs look set. Turn off the heat, add the sour cream, give the eggs a stir, and serve the mess directly out of the pan, with salsa on the side if you'd like.

SALSA

MAKES 3 CUPS

4 plum tomatoes, cut into ⅛-inch dice

1 teaspoon minced chili or jalapeño pepper

¼ red onion, cut into small dice

2 tablespoons coarsely chopped cilantro

Juice of 1 lime

½ teaspoon kosher salt

MIX ALL THE INGREDIENTS in a bowl and serve.

You can always top the break-fast mess with store-bought salsa, but it's so easy to make a fresh batch, why not try? This one tastes best when it's made ahead and refrigerated for a day.

PARTY TRICK

Make up a double batch of salsa and keep it on hand—you won't be sorry. Add it to mashed avocado for instant guacamole. Create a quick fajita party by serving it with grilled steak and soft tortillas. Combine it with rice and chicken for simple arroz con pollo. And definitely save some for snacking with chips.

PEANUT BUTTER AND JELLY YOGURT

SERVES 12

Three 32-ounce containers plain yogurt

One 18-ounce container peanut butter

3 cups of your favorite flavor jelly or jam (about four 12-ounce jars)

COMBINE ALL OF THE INGREDIENTS in a bowl. Stir to combine, but leave a few streaks of peanut butter and jelly.

The same perfect combination of a PB & J sandwich, but yogurt is substituted for the bread. Have the kids mix it up themselves; they'll love it.

PINEAPPLE, STRAWBERRY, AND BANANA SALAD

SERVES 12

1 pineapple, cut into small chunks

1 pound strawberries, stems removed, cut into thirds (halved if small)

5 bananas, sliced

A successful fruit salad depends on the right fruit combination, and this classic trio is one of my favorites.

COMBINE ALL THE ingredients in a bowl and serve immediately. (Or, if you want to prepare the salad ahead of time, cut the pineapple and strawberries and wait until the last minute to slice the bananas so they don't turn brown.)

Conventional WISDOM
A simple fruit salad isn't fancy enough to serve to guests.

real life WISDOM
Nothing beats a good combination of fresh seasonal fruit. You don't need any toppings or additions: Just pick the ripest fruit you can find, cut it up, and put it in a pretty bowl.

lunch BUFFETS

THE essentials

THE BASIC CONCEPT

There's something about entertaining during the day that feels more elegant, almost from another era. Often it works well with only women or only men, and it's a great time for bridal or baby showers, family gatherings, or other intimate celebrations. Still, that's no excuse to get fussy. The lunches in this chapter are not intended to be long drawn-out affairs, but simple modern meals that are unbelievably easy to prepare. You can just run home, throw them together, then sit with everyone to enjoy a delicious moment in the middle of the day.

Instead of spending time setting up a buffet, serve these lunches right out of the kitchen or—in the case of the Italian Street Fair Lunch—directly from the grill. Put out a stack of napkins, plates, and silverware, and let everyone help themselves. Choose a spot where everyone can sit, and mark it with some glasses and a big pitcher of iced tea. Help yourself to some food and join the others—there's nothing left for you to do.

IDEAL NUMBER OF GUESTS

8

WHO TO INVITE

A group of people who really have something in common. Some examples: your favorite girlfriends, a bunch of family members, everyone on your tennis team, a close group of coworkers.

MINIMUM ACCEPTABLE ADVANCE NOTICE

At least a week—sometimes it's hard for people to fit daytime events into their schedules.

WHAT TO TELL YOUR FRIENDS TO BRING

If you're celebrating something (or someone) in particular, definitely have everyone bring gifts. To avoid pressure, put a cap on expenditures—it'll make everyone more creative.

SETTING THE MOOD

Even though I never consider flowers mandatory, there's just something about lunch parties that screams out for flowers. Create low arrangements for the table with different flowers of the same color—and get creative with the vases. Little jelly jars are my favorite makeshift solution.

DRINK OF CHOICE

Iced tea or water

ULTIMATE SIGN OF SUCCESS

Major bonding

WHY I COOK THE MEALS IN THIS CHAPTER

It's hard to find the time for major preparations in the middle of the day, so each of these menus offers a solution for the time-crunched. The Salad Trifecta consists of a few elegant salads that can be prepared completely ahead of time, with just a little last-minute assembly. The Italian Street Fair Lunch shows how easy it is to throw together a hearty mixed grill. And if New York's ladies who lunch knew how easy the Park Avenue Luncheon was to prepare, they'd never eat out again.

SALAD trifecta

POACHED CHICKEN WITH TARRAGON PESTO

SERVES 8

1 tablespoon plus ½ teaspoon
kosher salt

8 large boneless, skinless chicken
breasts

1 cup extra virgin olive oil

Leaves from 8 tarragon sprigs

1 bunch parsley, thickest stems
removed

1 cup (about 5 ounces) slivered
almonds

Juice of 1½ lemons

¼ teaspoon freshly ground black
pepper

PLACE 4 INCHES OF WATER in a wide, deep pan with 1 tablespoon of the
salt and bring to a boil. Add the chicken breasts, and when the water returns to
a boil, reduce to a simmer, cover, and cook until they are firm and opaque
throughout, 20 to 25 minutes. Meanwhile, combine the olive oil, tarragon, parsley, almonds, lemon juice, pepper, and remaining salt in a blender or food processor to make the pesto. Pulse on high for about 30 seconds until a rough
paste has formed. When the chicken is cooked, remove from the water and let
cool until you are able to handle it comfortably. Slice the chicken ½ inch thick
across the grain. Drizzle with a little of the pesto and serve with the remaining
pesto in a bowl alongside.

Basil pesto is a classic, but I
love experimenting with
different herbs. Try making
this one with chives, chervil,
sorrel, or even celery leaves in
place of the tarragon. If you
feel like it, make a double
batch and spread it on sandwiches all week long.

PARTY TRICK

When you're serving a buffet where people are going to have to eat standing up,
make sure that everything is in bite-sized pieces so no one has to balance a plate,
fork, and knife.

ROASTED CORN, TOFU, AND BASIL SALAD

SERVES 8

8 ears corn, shucked

⅓ cup extra virgin olive oil

14 ounces extra-firm tofu, cut into ½-inch cubes

2½ tablespoons finely chopped basil

1 teaspoon kosher salt

½ teaspoon freshly ground black pepper

1 teaspoon red pepper flakes, optional

PREHEAT THE OVEN to 400°F.

PLACE THE CORN on a sheet pan and rub with 3 tablespoons of the olive oil. Place it in the oven and roast until fragrant and some of the kernels are golden brown, about 30 minutes. Remove and let cool. Hold each ear vertically over a bowl and slice the kernels off with a large knife. Add the remaining olive oil and the rest of the ingredients to the bowl and stir to combine.

Tofu is one of those ingredients that people always associate with depressing vegetarian food, but it actually makes a great protein in salads and sandwiches. It takes on the flavor of whatever it's mixed with—in this case, the super summer duo of corn and basil.

TOMATO, AVOCADO, AND CILANTRO SALAD

SERVES 8

16 plum tomatoes (about 2 pounds), cut into ½-inch chunks

4 Hass avocados, peeled and cut into ½-inch chunks

¼ cup roughly chopped cilantro

Juice of 4 limes

3 to 4 jalapeños, finely chopped

2 teaspoons kosher salt

1 teaspoon freshly ground black pepper

COMBINE ALL THE INGREDIENTS in a serving bowl and toss.

The hardest part about making this salad is getting the avocados just right. If you have time, buy hard avocados and leave them out to ripen for a few days until they're a little soft to the touch but not too mushy. If you're not yet ready to use them when they're just right, put them in the fridge and they'll stay that way for a few days.

MIDDLE EASTERN beauty

MEDITER-
RANEAN
SALAD

SESAME-MINT
PITA CHIPS

KIBBE
CORONAS

KIBBE CORONAS

SERVES 8

3 pounds ground beef

1 small onion, grated

¾ cup plain bread crumbs

1 tablespoon ground cumin

1 tablespoon kosher salt

1 tablespoon freshly ground black pepper

1 teaspoon ground cinnamon

½ teaspoon cayenne pepper

Inspired by a very popular Middle Eastern chopped lamb dish (and named after those fat, squat cigars called Coronas), these little logs of love are oh-so-easy to make and even better to eat. Their flavor is a little aromatic and ever so slightly spicy.

PREHEAT THE OVEN to 375°F. Cover a sheet pan with aluminum foil.

PLACE ALL THE INGREDIENTS in a bowl and mix until they're just combined, being careful not to overmix. Scoop up a handful of the mixture about the size of a Ping-Pong ball, then roll it into a short log and place it on the foil-covered sheet pan. Repeat with the remaining meat mixture (you should end up with about 24 logs). Place the sheet pan in the oven and bake for 10 minutes.

PARTY TRICK

With naturally beautiful food, the rustic look is perfect: throw everything in a bowl and presto, instant gorgeous. But when food is ugly (like these brown logs), making it look appealing requires a little more creativity. A geometric arrangement is the way to go: Here I've stacked the coronas in a pyramid. For other foods, try circles, squares, or lines. These shapes make your guests focus on the pattern more than on what it's made of.

MEDITERRANEAN SALAD

SERVES 8

Two 16-ounce cans garbanzo beans, drained and rinsed

8 plum tomatoes, cut into ¼-inch dice

3 cucumbers, peeled, quartered, and sliced ¼ inch thick

2 red bell peppers, cored, seeded, and cut into ¼-inch pieces

½ red onion, thinly sliced

4 scallions (both green and white parts), trimmed and thinly sliced

5 radishes, thinly sliced

3 tablespoons finely chopped dill

¾ cup white vinegar

1½ teaspoons sugar

¼ cup extra virgin olive oil

1 teaspoon kosher salt

COMBINE ALL THE INGREDIENTS except the salt in a serving bowl and mix to combine. Just before serving add the salt and mix well (if you add it earlier, the salad will get too wet).

My friend Jonathan Morr taught me how to make this salad, and it's become one of my summer staples. The vinegar and sugar combine to create a lightly pickled flavor, which goes perfectly with Middle Eastern–inspired dishes or just about anything from the grill. Serve it with a slotted spoon, since the salad gets juicier as it sits.

SESAME-MINT PITA CHIPS

SERVES 8

Four 6-inch pitas (one 8-ounce package)

¼ cup extra virgin olive oil

1 teaspoon ground cumin

1 tablespoon dried mint

1 tablespoon dried thyme

1 tablespoon sesame seeds

1 teaspoon red pepper flakes

½ teaspoon kosher salt

These are completely addictive! Try them with hummus, too.

PREHEAT THE OVEN to 375°F.

SPLIT THE WHOLE PITAS into eight rounds. Stack them, then cut the stacks into quarters. Place the pita slices in a single layer on a sheet pan (use two pans if they don't fit comfortably). Sprinkle with the olive oil, cumin, mint, thyme, sesame seeds, red pepper flakes, and salt. Place in the oven and cook, without turning, for 4 to 5 minutes. Remove and serve.

ITALIAN STREET FAIR lunch

With a rich dish like sausage (especially at lunch), you don't need to go the usual meat-starch-veggie route. Think of the peppers and onions as a freebie side dish.

ESCAROLE SALAD WITH ANCHOVY-LEMON DRESSING

GRILLED SAUSAGES, PEPPERS, AND ONIONS

GRILLED SAUSAGES, PEPPERS, AND ONIONS

SERVES 12

18 sausages links, hot, sweet, or a combination

6 bell peppers (any color), cored, seeded, and quartered

6 onions, peeled and quartered

Dijon mustard

This classic combination, straight from the street fairs of my childhood, involves nothing more than buying good sausages, slicing the vegetables, and putting someone willing in charge of the grill.

PREPARE A MEDIUM-HOT GRILL. Place as many of the ingredients as you can on the grill (except the mustard, of course). Cook, turning occasionally, until the sausages are charred and cooked through and the peppers and onions are charred and a little wilted, about 15 minutes. Throw on another batch if you need to, then serve with some good Dijon mustard alongside.

ESCAROLE SALAD WITH ANCHOVY-LEMON DRESSING

SERVES 12

1 ounce anchovies (about 6), finely chopped

1 teaspoon Dijon mustard

Juice of 1 lemon

¼ cup extra virgin olive oil

1 head escarole, cleaned

IN A SALAD BOWL, combine the anchovies, mustard, and lemon juice. Slowly add the olive oil, stirring well to combine. Add the leaves from the escarole, toss, and serve.

Even when it's the middle of winter and all the other lettuces at the supermarket look like they just fell off the back of a truck, escarole is the supermodel of leafy greens. It has a great crunch and a delicious, subtle bitterness that goes perfectly with anchovies.

PARTY TRICK

When you're entertaining more people than usual, you may not have platters that are big enough to hold everything. Get creative. Use vases, place mats, cutting boards, candy dishes, and anything else you can scrounge up around the house. Bread in a vase is one of my favorite makeshift solutions.

PARK AVENUE luncheon

Cooking the salmon and zucchini together saves you the trouble of making a separate vegetable side.

ALUMINUM-FOIL SALMON AND ZUCCHINI

SERVES 8

1 tablespoon extra virgin olive oil

One 2¼- to 2½-pound salmon fillet

3 zucchini, cut lengthwise into quarters, then thinly sliced

½ cup dry white wine

1 teaspoon kosher salt

½ teaspoon freshly ground black pepper

1 tablespoon butter, cut into small pieces

6 fresh thyme sprigs

¼ cup chopped parsley

You can make up this package the day before and put it in the oven whenever you're ready. The salmon steams away inside its aluminum-foil envelope while the zucchini cooks to a perfect al dente.

PREHEAT THE OVEN to 375°F. On a sheet pan, place four strips of aluminum foil with the shiny side down, two going one way and two going the other. Grease the inside of the foil with the olive oil.

PLACE THE SALMON, skin-side down, on the prepared pan, with the zucchini scattered around it. Pour the white wine on top, then sprinkle with the salt and pepper. Dot the salmon with the butter, then place the thyme sprigs on top. Sprinkle the whole pan with the parsley. Seal the salmon tightly by folding the aluminum foil into a tent. Cook for 12 minutes. Bring it to the table, carefully cut open the foil, and serve.

POTATOES AND CAVIAR

SERVES 8

10 medium Yukon gold potatoes	**½ cup salmon roe**
1½ cups sour cream	**1 tablespoon finely chopped chives**

BRING WATER TO A BOIL in the bottom of a pot with a steamer insert. Place the potatoes in the steamer basket and steam for 25 to 30 minutes until very tender. Transfer to a serving platter, being careful to space them at least 3 inches apart (they'll spread). With a small plate, press down on each potato until it breaks open and flattens. Top each potato with a dollop of sour cream, then evenly divide the salmon roe on top. Sprinkle with chives and serve.

You know those precious miniature potatoes filled with caviar you see passed at fancy cocktail parties? Well, this is their more rustic cousin. Using my all-time favorite Yukon gold potatoes and affordable (but still oh-so-tasty) salmon roe instead of Beluga, this dish is even more scrumptious than its black-tie relative. If you can't find salmon roe, top the sour cream with diced tomatoes, fresh dill, or even just a sprinkling of freshly ground black pepper.

one-pot MEALS

THE essentials

THE BASIC CONCEPT

Instead of worrying about salads, main dishes, side dishes, and all the other things that compose a normal meal, why not dump the concept of "normal" altogether and go for something much easier? In a single pot, you can create a dish that's exciting for your guests, ultra-easy for you, and of course no bother at all in the dishwashing department. It can be a thick, gorgeous vegetable-based soup, a big pot of meatballs in sauce, a really hearty chicken noodle soup, or a giant pot of steaming mussels cooked in that most nutritious of all beverages, beer. Just bring the whole big pot to the table, put out a loaf of crusty bread, and let everyone dig in.

Best of all, you don't even have to make these dishes on the spot. You can prepare all of these one-pot meals most of the way the day before, put the pot in the refrigerator, then take it out and finish cooking when you're almost ready for dinner. The hardest part of these meals just might be finding space in the fridge.

IDEAL NUMBER OF GUESTS
8 to 16

WHO TO INVITE
Anyone, especially in the winter-time, when we all crave these kinds of meals

MINIMUM ACCEPTABLE ADVANCE NOTICE
None

WHAT TO TELL YOUR FRIENDS TO BRING
Ask one friend to pick up a couple of loaves of crusty bread, and someone else to bring some extra spoons and bowls if you don't have enough.

SETTING THE MOOD
It's essential to serve these dishes straight from the pot, since bringing the food right to the table gives the evening a wonderfully rustic, generous feeling. Put out a good, thick trivet, set down your masterpiece, and start ladling away.

DRINK OF CHOICE
You can always stick with wine, but I love the conviviality of beer or hard cider for a one-pot meal.

ULTIMATE SIGN OF SUCCESS
An empty pot

WHY I COOK THE MEALS IN THIS CHAPTER
They're the essence of home-made food, derived from the simplest cooking technique of all—putting a pot over a fire. Some, like the Butternut Squash and Barley Soup, take a while to cook, but don't require much effort from you. Others, like the Mussels in Beer, are quick-cooking wonders. All of them have a homey, substantial feeling, and make everyone around the table feel deeply nurtured.

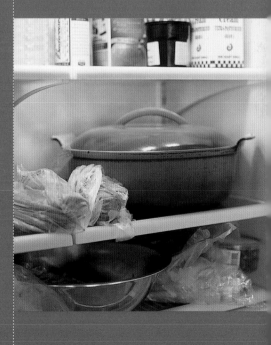

BUTTERNUT SQUASH AND BARLEY SOUP

SERVES 16

1 turkey wing

1 large butternut squash, peeled, seeded, and cut into 2-inch chunks

4 celery stalks, cut into ½-inch pieces

4 carrots, cut into ½-inch pieces

1 onion, cut into ½-inch wedges

5 parsley sprigs

6 sage leaves, plus 1 tablespoon finely chopped sage

1½ cups barley

2 teaspoons kosher salt

1 teaspoon freshly ground black pepper

PLACE THE TURKEY WING, squash, celery, carrots, onion, parsley, and whole sage in a large soup pot with 16 cups (1 gallon) of water, and place over high heat. When it comes to a boil, reduce to a simmer and cook for 45 minutes. (If you're going to refrigerate the soup, let it cool now, then bring it back up to simmer before proceeding.) Add the barley and cook for another 45 minutes. Just before serving, add the salt, pepper, and chopped sage, and stir.

Here's a soup that really takes care of itself. As the squash cooks, it breaks down into a thick, vibrant puree without ever going into the blender or getting mashed by hand. Instead of using canned or homemade stock, throw a turkey wing right into the pot to add flavor. If you can't find a wing, a drumstick will work, too.

Conventional WISDOM

One-pot meals are for supercasual family nights at home.

real life WISDOM

Everyone loves the hominess of one-pot meals. Have the courage to serve them to anyone—with a big hunk of bread alongside, you can't go wrong.

MEATBALLS AND TOMATO SAUCE

SERVES 8 TO 10

¼ cup extra virgin olive oil

5 garlic cloves, chopped

Two 28-ounce cans crushed tomatoes

1 teaspoon red pepper flakes

1½ pounds ground beef

1½ pounds ground pork

½ cup ricotta

3 large eggs

½ cup bread crumbs

1 teaspoon kosher salt

½teaspoon freshly ground black pepper

½ teaspoon ground nutmeg

10 basil leaves, chopped

How can something so perfect be this easy to make? There are two secret ingredients: The ricotta makes the meatballs light and a little tangy, and the nutmeg gives them a really subtle aromatic flavor.

PLACE A WIDE, heavy-bottomed pan over medium heat. When the pan is hot, add the olive oil and garlic. Let the garlic cook, stirring occasionally, 1 to 2 minutes, until it becomes fragrant and starts to turn golden. Add the tomatoes, being careful that they don't splatter on you. Add the red pepper flakes. Increase the heat to high, and when the mixture comes to a boil, reduce it to a simmer. Cook for 20 minutes, stirring occasionally. In a bowl, combine the beef, pork, ricotta, eggs, bread crumbs, salt, pepper, and nutmeg. Mix very lightly with your hands, just to combine, and then form into balls the size of a tennis ball. As you form each one, just drop it into the tomato sauce. Let the meatballs cook for 20 minutes, then carefully turn them and cook for another 20 minutes, occasionally stirring the sauce between the meatballs, just to make sure that nothing is sticking to the bottom of the pot. (If you're going to refrigerate the meatballs, let them cool and do it now. Add a cup of water to the sauce before reheating to make sure that nothing sticks.) Sprinkle with basil and serve.

PARTY TRICK

Kids love working with their hands, and meatball-making is a great excuse to involve them in the cooking effort. Show them how to make one, then ask them to follow suit. A bonus: Chances are good if you involve them now, they'll eat the meatballs later. Children will try almost anything if they've had a role in preparing it.

CHICKEN IN THE POT

SERVES 8

Two 2½- to 3-pound chickens, each cut into 8 pieces (or just 16 pieces of whatever chicken parts you like)

8 carrots, cut into 2-inch pieces

6 celery stalks, cut into 2-inch pieces

2 large onions, cut into eighths

5 dried bay leaves

5 sprigs parsley

Salt and pepper

One 12-ounce bag egg noodles

1 tablespoon chopped fresh dill

This dish just screams "home-made." Think of a steaming pot with lots of chicken, big chunks of veggies, and loads of egg noodles: my idea of heaven. The sprinkle of dill on top comes from my grandmother Frieda.

PLACE THE CHICKEN, carrots, celery, onions, bay leaves, parsley, and salt and pepper to taste in a large pot with 16 cups (1 gallon) of water. Place the pot over high heat, and when it comes to a boil, reduce to a simmer. Cook for 1 hour. (If you're going to refrigerate the chicken, let it cool and do it now.) When you're ready to serve, remove the bay leaves, place the pot over high heat, and when it comes to a boil, add the egg noodles. Cook for a minute less than the lowest number on the package directions. When it's ready, sprinkle with dill and serve immediately, directly from the pot.

NOTE: If you're not going to use the whole dish at once, just boil some noodles in the part you plan to use (the noodles get really mushy if you leave them in the soup).

PARTY TRICK

When it comes to protecting your table from a steaming-hot pot, a pot holder or folded dish towel will certainly do the trick, but my favorite trivets are actually tiles. I love cork tiles—you can find them at almost any craft store—or colorful ceramic ones. Just make sure they're totally flat so the pot remains stable.

MUSSELS IN BEER

SERVES 8

5 pounds mussels, debearded

1 bottle dark beer

1 head garlic, peeled and sliced

1 bunch parsley, roughly chopped

2 teaspoons coarsely ground black pepper

1 loaf crusty bread

PLACE ALL THE INGREDIENTS except the bread in a pot. (If you're going to refrigerate the mussels, do it now.) When you're ready, place the pot over a high flame and cook, covered, for 2 minutes. Give the pot a shake and cook 3 minutes more until all the mussels are open. If any refuse to open, discard them. Serve straight from the pot with a loaf of crusty bread.

This is a great summertime meal. Just bring the whole pot to the table, and make sure to have plenty of crusty bread on hand for dipping. (And some Wet-Naps too, if you don't plan to go in the pool right away.)

To debeard mussels, run them under water and pull the strand that looks like steel wool out of the shells. Some stores may have mussels that are already debearded (if you find them, lucky you)!

PARTY TRICK

If you want to skip utensils altogether for this meal, go right ahead. Just show everyone how to go fork-free by using an empty mussel shell as tongs to pinch out a fresh mussel. After they're done eating, your guests can use the empty shell as a spoon to scoop up the broth.

dinner for a CROWD

THE essentials

THE BASIC CONCEPT

Okay, these are the big blowouts. There is a bunch of people you've been meaning to invite over for ages, and you're finally going to do it. Or maybe it's someone's birthday or anniversary or other big occasion. Don't panic. Just because the number of guests is large and the occasion important, don't think you have to pull out all the stops, hire a bartender, or worry about place cards.

Entertaining a larger crowd than usual will require some makeshift solutions. Some people might have to sit on the floor. A friend can come a little early to open the wine. You might need to borrow a platter or ask a friend to bring a few extra serving spoons. All of that is okay. In fact, it brings the people you've invited even closer to you. They're participating, not just attending, and that's the whole point.

IDEAL NUMBER OF GUESTS
8 to 12

WHO TO INVITE
If it's a particular occasion, the guest list should be obvious. Otherwise, tell each of your friends to bring someone you don't know. It's a great way of expanding your social circle, and it always makes for a really interesting party.

MINIMUM ACCEPTABLE ADVANCE NOTICE
3 days

WHAT TO TELL YOUR FRIENDS TO BRING
I often ask people to bring a specific wine varietal that's easy to find, like Chianti or Pinot Noir. The party becomes an impromptu wine tasting. And no, you don't need separate glasses for each wine; that's way too stuffy for real life entertaining.

SETTING THE MOOD
Instead of worrying about flowers and candles, think about yourself. There's nothing that sets quite as festive a tone as a host who's made a real effort. Wear something a little outrageous: I might stick some bright pink fake flowers or a tiara in my hair, or put on a scandalously short skirt. Choose something that goes with your personality and the party will buzz the minute your guests walk in the door.

DRINK OF CHOICE
Wine, wine, and more wine! And perhaps a little dessert wine afterward, too.

ULTIMATE SIGN OF SUCCESS
You can't get anyone to leave.

WHY I COOK THE MEALS IN THIS CHAPTER
When you're making dinner for a large group, every dish has to be easy to make, a general crowd-pleaser, and not too effort-intensive for the cook. You're looking for surefire recipes—the ones here are the dishes I prepare again and again when I want the evening to come off without a hitch. The Roasted Chicken Legs with Mustard and Thyme is a one-pan, one-hour wonder. Texas London Broil uses one of the most inexpensive cuts of beef, which, with the right seasonings and accompaniments, feels like a feast. Roasted Pork Tenderloins with Apples is a dressed-up riff on the classic American pork chops and applesauce—and another one-pan miracle.

so south-of-france

ROASTED CHICKEN LEGS WITH MUSTARD AND THYME

SERVES 8

3 large shallots, finely chopped

1 cup grainy Dijon mustard

1 cup Dijon mustard

¼ cup extra virgin olive oil

1 teaspoon freshly ground black pepper

1½ cups dry white wine

20 (about 6 pounds) chicken drumsticks

15 thyme sprigs

This dish tastes like one you'd get in a bistro in France, but all you have to do is put the ingredients in a roasting pan and throw it in the oven.

PREHEAT THE OVEN to 375°F.

PLACE THE SHALLOTS, mustards, olive oil, pepper, and white wine on a sheet pan and stir together to combine. Add the chicken and thyme sprigs and toss to coat. Spread out into a single layer and roast in the oven for 1 hour. Transfer to a serving bowl, carefully scraping the sauce from the pan into the bowl. Toss to coat.

Conventional WISDOM

A proper meal should be served in courses, with an appetizer, an entrée, and dessert.

real life WISDOM

Who cares about being proper? The most important thing you can do as a host is spend time with your guests, and you'll never be able to do that if you're constantly shuttling back and forth to the kitchen. Instead of going for restaurant-like formality, just put everything on the table at once, and let people serve themselves at a pace they—and you—enjoy.

WILD MUSHROOM CROUTON SALAD

SERVES 8

½ cup extra virgin olive oil

1 loaf (about 1 pound) crusty country bread, cut into ¾-inch cubes

2 large garlic cloves, finely chopped

2 pounds mixed mushrooms (domestic, wild, or exotic), stemmed and sliced ¼ inch thick

Salt and pepper

½ cup coarsely chopped parsley

With a deep, woodsy flavor, this winter-friendly side goes well with roasted meats, too.

PLACE A WIDE, heavy-bottomed pan over medium-high heat. When the pan is hot, add ¼ cup of the olive oil, then the bread. Cook, stirring occasionally, until the bread is golden brown, about 10 minutes. Empty into a bowl. Return the pan to the heat and add the remaining olive oil and garlic. When the garlic just starts to become fragrant, about 2 minutes, add the mushrooms and cook until some of the liquid is released and they are softened but still maintain their shape, about 10 minutes. Remove the pan from the heat, add the salt and pepper to taste, and the parsley, and stir well to combine. (If you aren't going to serve the dish immediately, set the mushrooms aside. Continue when you're almost ready to sit down.) Add the croutons back to the pan and toss again. Serve immediately.

PARTY TRICK

Yes, it's true, even shy people can enjoy entertaining. Try this trick: Walk around with a wine bottle in hand, offering refills to everyone. It's a great way to start a conversation—and everyone always wants to talk to the host if you just give them an excuse.

SIMPLE SALAD

SERVES 8

1 tablespoon Dijon mustard

1 tablespoon red wine vinegar

⅓ cup or more extra virgin olive oil

8 ounces mixed greens or 1 head green leaf lettuce

IN A SALAD BOWL, combine the mustard and vinegar and stir with a spoon. Slowly drizzle in the olive oil a little at a time, stirring vigorously and adding more only after the previously added oil has been completely incorporated. The mixture should maintain a thick consistency. Taste it, and if it's too tangy, slowly add another tablespoon or two of olive oil. Add the greens and toss well.

I make the vinaigrette for this salad almost every day of my life. When I'm home for lunch, I love using it on salad greens with a bunch of different vegetables and leftover chicken or meat. When artichokes are in season, I steam a couple and use the vinaigrette as a dipping sauce. It's quite thick, which makes it a perfect dip for raw vegetables, too.

Conventional WISDOM

No dinner is complete without a cooked vegetable.

real life WISDOM

Salad makes a great vegetable dish, and it's one more thing you don't have to worry about cooking.

MEXICAN madness

TEXAS LONDON BROIL

SERVES 12

Three 1¼-pound London broil
steaks, about 1 inch thick

2 tablespoons extra virgin olive oil

2 teaspoons ground cumin

2 teaspoons dried oregano

1 teaspoon ground thyme

1 teaspoon cayenne pepper

2 teaspoons kosher salt

1 teaspoon freshly ground black
pepper

For my mother, who loves
inexpensive cuts of meat with
tons of flavor, London broil is
the holy grail. Allow the meat
to rest and then slice it very
thinly against the grain.

PREHEAT THE OVEN to 375°F.

PLACE THE LONDON BROIL on a sheet pan and drizzle it with the olive oil.
Rub the oil onto the meat. Sprinkle all the remaining ingredients on all sides.
Place the meat in the oven and roast for 10 minutes. Turn and cook for another
6 minutes. Let the meat rest for 5 minutes, then slice it superthin against the
grain. Spoon the juices over the meat and serve.

PARTY TRICK

Instead of serving cocktails when guests first walk in, then switching to wine at the
table, pour your friends a glass of wine when they walk in the door and have them
bring their glasses to the table for dinner.

EASY GUACAMOLE

MAKES 2 CUPS

3 Hass avocados, soft and ripe

Juice of 2 limes

½ small red onion, finely chopped

1 to 2 jalapeños, finely chopped

¼ cup chopped cilantro

1 teaspoon kosher salt

¼ teaspoon freshly ground black pepper

SLICE THE AVOCADOS IN HALF. Remove the pits and scoop the flesh into a bowl. Add the remaining ingredients and stir well to combine. Serve with tortilla chips.

I never understand why people buy premade guacamole. There's nothing easier to make at home, and the results are so much better. Keep in mind that unlike the preservative-packed store-bought variety, home-made guacamole will discolor over time. Pressing a piece of plastic wrap directly on top of the guacamole before wrapping it and putting it in the fridge will keep it green for up to 24 hours.

SPICY PINEAPPLE SALSA

SERVES 12

1 pineapple, cut into ⅛-inch dice

6 plum tomatoes, cut into ⅛-inch dice

½ cup finely chopped cilantro

3 jalapeños, seeded and finely chopped

Juice of 4 limes

1½ teaspoons kosher salt

2 teaspoons freshly ground black pepper

COMBINE ALL THE INGREDIENTS in a bowl and stir well. Let the salsa sit for a few hours, if possible.

Salsa can be made with many different fruits and vegetables, and this tropical version is a great example. Try it with London broil, tortilla chips, or a smoked turkey sandwich. It keeps well in the refrigerator, too, and actually gets better after a few days.

GREEN RICE

SERVES 12

5 jalapeños, seeded

20 cilantro sprigs, stems removed

1 bunch parsley, stems removed

4 garlic cloves

2 cups basmati or Texmati rice

1 tablespoon kosher salt

1 teaspoon freshly ground black pepper

2 tablespoons extra virgin olive oil

PLACE THE JALAPEÑOS, cilantro, parsley, garlic, and 2 cups of water in a blender or food processor and blend on high for 10 seconds, or until all the ingredients are well chopped and the water is green. Place this mixture in a large pot with the rice, salt, pepper, olive oil, and an additional 1½ cups water. Place over high heat and stir to combine. When it comes to a boil, reduce to a simmer, cover tightly, and cook—without peeking—for 15 minutes. Let it sit for 10 minutes, fluff with a fork, and serve.

The aromatic, nutty basmati rice in this dish gets a major kick from a spicy, herb-packed cooking broth. The result is a bright green wonder, perfect for any meal with a Tex-Mex bent. Wrap up any leftovers in a big tortilla with black beans and shredded Cheddar for an instant vegetarian burrito.

PARTY TRICK

To keep tortillas warm, place a damp dishcloth on a plate, put the warm tortillas inside it, and fold it over.

SOUTHERN *love*

ROASTED PORK TENDERLOINS AND APPLES

SERVES 8

½ cup Dijon mustard

½ cup brown sugar

1 teaspoon freshly ground black pepper

2 pork tenderloins, about 1¼ pounds each

4 red Delicious apples, cored (not peeled) and cut into quarters

Here's a simple twist on the all-American combination of pork chops and applesauce, made even easier by trading pork chops for two tender, easy-to-cook pork tenderloins. And instead of labor-intensive homemade applesauce, the apples are tossed into the pan to caramelize alongside the meat.

PREHEAT THE OVEN to 375°F. Cover a sheet pan with aluminum foil.

PLACE THE MUSTARD, brown sugar, and pepper in a mound in the middle of the sheet pan and mix well. Place the pork and apples on top and turn to coat everything. Spread out into a single layer. Place the pork and apples in the oven and roast, without turning, for 30 minutes. Serve, spooning some of the juices onto the meat.

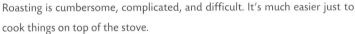

Conventional WISDOM

Roasting is cumbersome, complicated, and difficult. It's much easier just to cook things on top of the stove.

real life WISDOM

Roasting is a dream for entertaining. You prepare everything ahead of time, then put the pan in the oven whenever you're ready, leaving you plenty of time to spend with your friends when they arrive.

SAUTÉED SWISS CHARD

SERVES 8

6 tablespoons extra virgin olive oil

2 bunches Swiss chard, tough ends discarded, cut crosswise at 1-inch intervals

½ teaspoon kosher salt

½ teaspoon freshly ground black pepper

PLACE A LARGE, HEAVY-BOTTOMED PAN over very high heat. When you can see it starting to smoke, add one-third of the olive oil, one-third of the chard, and one-third of the salt and pepper. Cook, stirring occasionally, until the chard has softened but not completely wilted, about 3 minutes. Transfer to a bowl. Repeat this process twice more until all the chard is cooked. Return it all to the pan briefly to reheat, then bring the pan to the table and serve.

This chard is essentially stir-fried, giving it a great fresh, minerally taste and a lovely crunch. While many people think the leaves have to be removed from the stems, I like the crunchiness of leaving them on (and love eliminating the extra step).

Conventional WISDOM

Hors d'oeuvres are essential, and the more elaborate, the better.

real life WISDOM

There'll be plenty of food at dinner—the only reason to have something to eat beforehand is in case your guests are starving and that first glass of wine can go right to their heads. Save your efforts for the main meal, and put out some good roasted nuts or olives for the cocktail hour.

RED CABBAGE SLAW WITH LEMON AND DILL

SERVES 8 WITH PLENTY LEFT OVER

¼ cup buttermilk

½ cup sour cream

¾ cup mayonnaise

2 tablespoons chopped fresh dill

Zest of 2 lemons

3 tablespoons white vinegar

1 red cabbage, about 3 pounds, core removed, cut into ½-inch squares

COMBINE ALL THE INGREDIENTS except the cabbage in a large bowl and stir well. Add the cabbage and toss. If you have time, let the slaw sit for an hour or two to let the flavors develop. Otherwise, just go ahead and serve it.

Slaw is a terrific thing to put out on a big buffet. Unlike traditional salads, it keeps well for hours, and brings a bright, exciting flavor to whatever else you're serving. In this version, the lemon, dill, and buttermilk combine to create a tangy, herbal flavor that goes really well with the pork.

THE splurge

BEEF TENDERLOIN

SERVES 10 TO 12

One 4- to 5-pound whole beef
tenderloin, trimmed

1 teaspoon extra virgin olive oil

2 teaspoons kosher salt

2 teaspoons freshly ground black
pepper

Grainy Dijon mustard

PREHEAT THE OVEN to 425°F.

PLACE THE BEEF TENDERLOIN on a sheet pan and rub it with the olive oil.
Sprinkle on all sides with the salt and pepper. Place it in the oven and cook,
without turning, for 20 minutes (rare) to 25 minutes (medium). Let it sit for 10
minutes before carving. Serve with mustard on the side.

PARTY TRICK

A big party is not the time to spring for expensive wines. Visit your trusted local
wine store, tell them what you're serving, and mention that you're looking for a
good, cheap wine to go with it. Yes, use the C word—it takes all of the pretentious-
ness out of the equation, and often results in a terrific moderately priced find that
your salesperson is proud to have discovered and actually enjoys drinking.

While I'm an advocate of cooking with affordable ingredients, every once in a while, it pays to splurge. There's no better bang for your beef buck than whole tenderloin, the Rolls-Royce of the bovine world. Even though it's pricey, the quality is so outrageously obvious from the first bite (like butter!) that you—and especially your guests—will be thrilled you took the plunge.

EGGPLANT, TOMATO, AND RICOTTA STACKS

SERVES 10 TO 12

¼ cup extra virgin olive oil, plus
more for greasing the pans

1 large eggplant, sliced into fifteen
½-inch rounds

2 beefsteak tomatoes, cored and
sliced into fifteen ¼-inch rounds

One 15-ounce container fresh
ricotta

10 large basil leaves, finely shredded

1 teaspoon kosher salt

PREHEAT THE OVEN to 375°F. Grease two sheet pans with olive oil.

PLACE THE EGGPLANT in a single layer and sprinkle with the olive oil. Place one tomato round on top of each eggplant slice. Divide the ricotta evenly over the tomatoes. Bake for 25 minutes, sprinkle with basil, and return to the oven for another 5 minutes. The ricotta should be golden in places, and the basil should be crispy. Sprinkle with salt before serving.

These are as easy to make for a big crowd as they are for a little family dinner. You can assemble the vegetable stacks ahead of time, and bake them whenever you're ready. The cheese doesn't really melt, it just kind of collapses a bit, so these can be served piping hot or at room temperature.

TRICOLOR SALAD

SERVES 10 TO 12

2 bunches arugula, stems removed

3 heads endive, separated into leaves

1 head radicchio, sliced

Olive oil

Balsamic vinegar

Kosher salt

Pepper mill

ON A SERVING PLATTER or in a big bowl, arrange the arugula, endive, and radicchio. Place bottles of olive oil and balsamic vinegar alongside, with a little bowl of kosher salt and a pepper mill.

No matter how artistically challenged you think you are, this salad will look gorgeous. Just arrange the vegetables on a platter in three stripes like the Italian flag, and you're in business.

desserts

THE essentials

TO ME, the world is divided into people who bake and people who don't, and I am definitely in the latter category. All that precise measuring drives me crazy, as does putting something in the oven that I'm not going to interact with again until it's done. I like puttering around, stirring this and that, tasting a dish every step of the way, being involved. I guess baking is just a little too hands-off for my taste. And it's a very time-consuming and dirty bowl-making activity, which is a bad fit for how I prefer to entertain. If a guest says, "Let me bring dessert," I'm all for it.

But maybe you're not like me, and you like baking cookies, brownies, and pies. If that's the case, my advice is this: Build your parties around that passion. Invite people over for tea and cakes on a Saturday afternoon, or for dessert and champagne after a performance. Bring a homemade birthday cake with you to a party someone else has organized. Celebrate your talents, and don't bother with the things you don't like to do. Organize your entertaining to suit your passion and forget about the rest.

But what if you love baking *and* cooking, you talented devil? If so, I say go with it and do them both, but not at the same time. Even in a professional restaurant kitchen, the executive chef and the pastry chef are two different people with two different staffs. Don't take on the task of playing both roles for the same event in the limited time you have in your own kitchen. One week, throw a dessert party, and the next, have a bunch of friends over for dinner. Bring dessert when you're invited to a friend's house. Or bake desserts the day before your dinner parties, if you have time. Just make sure that every time you think about having a dinner party you're not defeated by the idea that you have to bake a cake, too.

Okay, so you're convinced (maybe) that it's just too much work to throw a dinner party *and* bake dessert from scratch. Good. Still, there's something that just feels wrong about ending a meal right after the main course. You can't just go from "pass the pork" to "have a safe trip home" without *something*. There are plenty of ways to end a meal that don't require baking. Turn the whole dessert course over to a guest, serve some store-bought goodies, or put out a few things that are a cinch to throw together. Here are some ideas.

DELEGATE

Ah, the glorious D-word! This is my favorite solution to the dessert problem. After asking most guests to bring a bottle of wine, I tell one person to pick up something for dessert. If the person happens to love baking, he or she can certainly whip up some pie or brownies or a cake, but otherwise, some cookies from a bakery or a couple of pints of ice cream from the supermarket are fine. I let the person know how many people are coming and encourage him or her to get something simple.

A little presumptuous, though, isn't it? Not at all. Don't feel as if you're imposing by asking your guests to bring something. You're actually giving your friends an opportunity to be a part of the evening. Just be sure to sing those friends' praises when dessert comes out!

A CHEESE **COURSE**

Cheese has all the richness and decadence of dessert, but without the sweetness. A cheese course traditionally has a selection of cheeses, but I prefer a simpler approach. I buy a big hunk of one cheese, and serve it on a wooden platter (usually my cutting board) with some crackers or sliced bread, and some dried fruit. And my favorite thing about cheese? It requires nothing more than being unwrapped, placed artfully on a tray, and allowed to come to room temperature. Some of my favorite combinations are (clockwise from right) Roquefort with figs, Manchego with apricots, goat cheese with dried currants, and aged Gouda with dates.

FRUIT AND **CHOCOLATE**

My favorite way to end a meal. I put out fruit that doesn't require a knife or even a plate (yes, even at the very end of the meal, after a few glasses of wine, I'm still thinking about how to cut down on the number of dishes!). A single kind of fruit looks so elegant and modern when piled high in a bowl. No matter what time of year there's usually at least one fruit that's in season. Arrange that fruit in a bowl, with a little ice on top if you'd like, and place a smaller, empty bowl alongside for the pits, stems, or peels. Some favorites include clementine oranges, grapes, apricots, cherries, small plums, and Seckel pears.

But still, I have some friends who are absolute chocoholics, and I don't like to see anyone go into fits around the table. So I always keep a couple of good chocolate bars in the freezer. To accompany the fruit bowl, I break a few bars into irregular shards and arrange them in a pretty dish. It looks elegant and is the perfect ending to any meal.

ICE CREAM WITH A QUICK SAUCE

Some occasions do require going a bit over the top. When I want to make something that doesn't take too much time or effort, but still has that "wow" effect at the end of the meal, I turn to my quick dessert sauces. They're great on any kind of ice cream (which, of course, you can always have a friend pick up on the way to your house) or on a store-bought pound cake. Bring everything out with a stack of bowls or mugs, and start dishing it out. Or give the job to the shyest person at the party for a boost of instant mega-popularity.

PINEAPPLE PEPPER SAUCE
MAKES ABOUT 1 CUP (SERVES 8 AS A TOPPING)

½ pineapple, cut into small pieces (about 2 cups)

½ cup sugar

1 teaspoon coarsely ground black pepper

PLACE ALL OF THE INGREDIENTS in a pan and place over high heat. When it comes to a boil, reduce to a simmer and cook for 30 minutes. Serve warm over ice cream.

It may sound like a crazy combination, but it works like a charm. For a fully tropical effect, serve this sauce over coconut ice cream.

RUM RAISIN SAUCE

MAKES ABOUT 1 CUP (SERVES 8 AS A TOPPING)

1 cup packed raisins

1 cup rum

½ cup packed brown sugar

PLACE ALL OF THE INGREDIENTS in a pan and place over high heat. When it comes to a boil, reduce to a simmer and cook for 20 minutes. Serve warm over ice cream.

You probably have the ingredients to make this in your kitchen right now, so go ahead and do it. There's nothing better on a scoop of vanilla.

VANILLA APRICOT SAUCE

MAKES ABOUT 1 CUP (SERVES 8 AS A TOPPING)

16 ounces (about 1 cup, packed) dried apricots, sliced

½ cup sugar

1 tablespoon vanilla extract

PLACE ALL OF THE INGREDIENTS in a pan with 1 cup water and place over high heat. When it comes to a boil, reduce to a simmer and cook for 15 minutes. Serve warm over ice cream.

APPLE PIE SAUCE

MAKES ABOUT 1 CUP (SERVES 8 AS A TOPPING)

1 large Granny Smith apple, peeled and cut into ⅛-inch dice

1 cup packed brown sugar

1 teaspoon ground cinnamon

½ teaspoon ground nutmeg

Juice of ½ lemon

Use any leftover sauce on French toast in the morning.

PLACE ALL OF THE INGREDIENTS in a pan with 1 cup water and place over high heat. When it comes to a boil, reduce to a simmer and cook for 45 minutes. Serve warm over ice cream.

LIQUID DESSERT

If dinner was heavy or particularly filling, a little nightcap instead
of dessert might not be a bad idea. Try serving after-dinner drinks
in pretty, mismatched glasses after you clear the main course. Not
everyone will be interested in a glass of grappa or dessert wine,
but it feels very generous and is a great way to end the meal.

PUTTING YOUR kitchen together

A LOT OF MY FRIENDS who have dream kitchens prepare 90 percent of their meals in the microwave. On the other hand, I've enjoyed some of the best home-cooked meals I've ever had from kitchens with only the most rudimentary equipment. The point is this: You're going to need some basic gear to put together good homemade meals, but you definitely don't need to own top-of-the-line equipment or the latest gadgets on the market.

My own kitchen is minimally equipped, and I use the same pots, pans, and utensils again and again. Look around your cupboards, make do with what you have, then pick up a new item when a recipe calls for it. A well-stocked kitchen doesn't happen in a day: It's the result of buying things as you go, expanding as necessary, and developing a well-worn set of equipment that's uniquely yours.

If you find yourself cooking all the time, you might want to invest in a heavy, solid chef's knife and a wide, heavy-bottomed pan, but don't worry about owning these right away. I didn't buy my first good knife until I'd been entertaining for ten years.

As for food processors and other supposed time-saving devices, I usually find that by the time I'm done assembling, disassembling, and cleaning them, I could just as easily have done it all by hand. Plus, there's something really calming and meditative about chopping, grating, and mixing the old-fashioned way. That said, if you have some gadgets that work for you, by all means go ahead and use them—you always know best.

Here's a list of what you might want to have in your kitchen. But remember: It's always better to make do with what you have than to not entertain at all.

EQUIPMENT

CHEF'S KNIFE. It should be big and heavy and feel good in your hand. If you're used to using small or low-quality knives, you'll be amazed by how much quicker you'll be able to cut once you upgrade. Eight to 10 inches is the best all-purpose size.

CUTTING BOARD. The flexible plastic kind is a snap to clean, but a wooden one can double as a rustic serving platter, a big bonus.

WIDE, HEAVY-BOTTOMED PAN. Someone once gave me this big, fabulous copper-bottomed pan, and I use it every day of my life (thank you, Susan!). It's the only pan you'll need for almost everything you cook on the stovetop, from stews to stir-fries to meatballs in tomato sauce. Look for one at least 10 inches wide, with a cover.

SHEET PANS. These aren't so commonly used in home kitchens, but walk into any restaurant in America and you'll see stacks and stacks of them. They're flat, rectangular, and aluminum-coated with a little lip. I use them for almost everything that goes in the oven, but if you don't have any, you can usually substitute a shallow roasting pan or cookie sheet.

WOODEN SPOONS. Buy a few in different sizes. They're the perfect kitchen utensil: time-tested, cheap, and incredibly versatile.

VEGETABLE PEELER. You can stick with the metal kind, but the newer ones with rubber handles make peeling *anything* a thousand times easier. I say splurge.

SALAD SPINNER. One of the most important pieces of equipment in a kitchen, since it's impossible to make a good salad without dry greens.

SPATULAS. One pancake-flipping version and one bowl-scraping version. The ones made from silicone won't burn even if you leave them in a hot pan.

COLANDER. In metal or plastic, it's essential for pasta and useful for draining just about anything.

PASTA POT WITH A STEAMER INSERT. The bigger, the better.

SMALL POT. Any 2- to 3-quart saucepan works for melting butter, boiling eggs, or heating up leftover soup.

MIXING BOWLS. Glass, metal, or ceramic are all fine. Buy a set of three in different sizes, and get pretty ones so you can bring them straight to the table.

BLENDER. For everything from smoothies to pesto. A food processor will work, too.

SMALL SAUTÉ PAN (6 to 8 inches). I love mine from Le Creuset, which would normally be a big-ticket item, but I found it at a thrift shop (always a great resource for kitchen bargains).

BOX GRATER. The classic kind is perfect for grating everything from carrots to Parmesan.

PARING KNIFE. Any small knife will do. I bought one ages ago for about $5 and it works wonders.

LADLE. Essential for everything from skimming soups to serving pasta.

SERRATED BREAD KNIFE. Makes cutting bread and slicing tomatoes a breeze.

GRILL PAN. An indoor alternative to barbecue.

PIE PLATE. You can live without it, but then you'd also have to live without quiche, and who would want to do that?

BREAD KNIFE

CHEF'S K

SPATULA

BLENDER

SALAD SPINNER

TONGS

PIE PLATE

PASTA POT

PARING KNIFE

PEELER

SPATULA

GRILL PAN

SHEE

CUTTING BOARD

LADLE

BOX GRATER

MIXING BOWL

MOM

COLANDER

SAUTÉ PAN

SLOTTED SPOON

WIDE, HEAVY-BOTTOMED PAN

index